Basics of Business

How to Run a Successful Business

By: Dave Young

Table of Contents

Introduction

Basics of Business is a perfect guide for anyone who wants to start a business or for those who are about to expand their current business. This book will give you all the information that you need to know before you start your business, and it will also teach you how to run your business efficiently. You will learn the essential aspects that you need to know when starting up a new business, as well as how to manage your employees and make your business grow. The book also addresses the methods that will help you succeed in your business. If you are interested in running a successful business, then this book is for you.

The Benefits of Reading This Book

By reading *Basics of Business - How to Run a Successful Business*, you will learn:

- How to start your own business or how to expand your current business.
- How to manage your employees.
- How to make your business grow.
- The methods that will help you succeed in your business.
- How to manage your time and money effectively.

And much more!

Chapter 1: Starting a Business – Your First Steps

In this chapter, we'll discuss some of the first steps you should take in starting your own business. This is a relatively simple process if you think about it, but there are some important steps that you need to take before you open your doors for business. We'll discuss some of those steps here.

What Is a Business?

Before we get into the discussion of how to start a business, let's talk about what a business is. A business can be generally defined as any activity or organization that makes money by providing goods and/or services to customers. The customer pays for the goods or services and is happy with their purchase. It is important that both parties feel good about their relationship and are willing to do it again in the future. Let's look at each of these parts separately and examine why they are important. First, let's look at the making money part of this definition.

A business sits down and plans out how it is going to make money. It may have a service, such as a dentist's office or an insurance company, or it may have a product, such as a toy store or a computer store. The business must have some idea of how they are going to make money if they are going to stay in business.

The business owner can have some sort of outside financing, such as from a bank or an investor, but most businesses must rely on customers to provide that financing. This means that the owner has to make sure that he/she can convince people they will like what the business has for sale and will want to purchase it from them again and again. This is called getting repeat business.

For this repeat business to happen, the customer needs to be happy with their purchase when they leave the store or when they leave the office. They need to feel good about the price they paid for the service and also about their experience in general with your company. If you have this repeat business with your customers, you can count on making money over and over again on your sales until your customer decides that it is time to shop elsewhere!

Choosing a Business

As I mentioned before, you must think about the type of business that you want to run. This is an American-made personal decision and should be based on your tastes in life. There are a lot of different things out there to sell and a lot of different ways to make money from these items. Let's take a look at some of the different types of businesses that you may want to consider.

You may want to think about starting your own business if any of the following applies to you:

- You are interested in starting your own business, and you do not want to work for someone else.

- You want more freedom, and you want to make more money.
- You have a skill or talent that can be turned into a business. For example, you can build and repair computers for people, or maybe you are good at putting together budgets for people and helping them with their finances. Maybe you are good at organizing things and can help a disorganized person clean up their office or home.
- You like working with people and would enjoy working in a business environment where there will always be customers coming in the front door.
- You like solving problems and trying out different things in creative ways.

If any of these situations apply to you, then it is possible that starting your own business is something you should consider doing! There are lots of books on this subject as well as courses on how to start your own business, so look around at what's out there before deciding what type of business and what type of product or service you want to provide.

Find a Market

The second step in starting a business is to find a market. A market[1] is defined as a group of people who are willing and able to pay money for your product or service. They must be organized so that you can reach them easily to

---

[1] Adam Hayes (updated February 23rd 2021) available from https://www.investopedia.com/terms/f/financial-market.asp

do business with them. They must have or be willing to spend money.

To find your market, you must first define your product. What are you selling? Once you have defined your product, you must decide how you are going to market it. This means deciding how you are going to get the word out about your product and how much it is going to cost for advertising and promotion. Once you have determined this, then you can determine who is in your market and what they need or want from a company like yours.

For example, if I am starting a new car dealership, I know that I am selling cars! But, what kind of cars? Will I sell only Toyotas or Chevys? Will I sell foreign or domestic cars? Am I going to sell sedans, trucks, or sports cars? Once I have answered these questions for myself then I can begin looking for the people who will buy my product from me.

I know that there are people who will buy Toyotas because they come with a great warranty and have been known to be very reliable as well as inexpensive to maintain. There may be some people who will only buy American-made cars, but most Americans tend not to care whether their car is American-made or not because it is probably cheaper to buy a foreign car, and I can compete on price with them. The reason I can compete with foreign cars on price is that they are made over in Japan, and this means that they do not require as many man-hours for production. They are also built in larger quantities, hence the lower cost.

As I look for my market, I know that there are people who want to buy cars but may not have the money to do so. These are the people who will need financing, which makes it an excellent opportunity for a car dealership to sell cars on credit! A dealer would not want to finance each car they sell, but they could earn enough extra money from their financing division that would make it worth their while.

I also know there are people who may want to lease a car instead of buying one outright. This lowers my customer's monthly payment and makes it easier for them to afford a new or near-new car without putting all of their money into it at once. As you can see, there are many opportunities in the marketplace! This makes me feel good about starting my new business because only a very small portion of my market is already taken up by other companies selling similar products! This means that I have a good chance of making money!

I may decide that I need to sell cars on a limited basis at first and expand my market later. For example, I may decide to sell only Toyotas at first, and then add Honda or Nissan later. You never know what your market wants unless you try to provide them with the goods or services they are looking for!

Now that we have discussed the basic components of a business, we can discuss how to start one. As you read this chapter, remember that there are many factors involved in starting your business, so this discussion of "how to start a business" is more of an overview of the process. Many details must be ironed out before you can successfully open your doors for business.

Plan Your Business

Planning your business is an important step that you must take before you open your doors and start selling. If you have a good plan in place, you will be able to make the most money in the least amount of time.

You should ask yourself what it is that you want to sell. You should also ask yourself who it is that you want to sell to. When you answer these questions, you can begin to plan your business. For example, if you want to sell snakes as pets, then where are people going to buy them? Are they going to buy them online, or will they go into a pet store and purchase them there?

Once you know where your customer will buy their snakes or whatever it is that you are interested in selling, the next step would be for the owner of the business to find out what kinds of snakes are people are interested in buying. Is there a certain type of snake that everyone wants? Or does the preference differ from person to person? This information will help determine how much inventory (snakes) the owner should begin with and how many he/she should order at any given time. If everyone wants red snakes and there aren't any left, then the owner will need to order some more. He/she will also need to make sure that he/she doesn't run out of red snakes at a time when people want them.

If you are selling a product, such as a software program, then you'll need to find out how many people are interested in buying your product. If there is not much interest in the program, it may be best for you to try and sell something else. Maybe you should sell a different type of software program or a different product entirely. You may even want to consider selling your services rather than having a product for sale.

For example, if you are a computer programmer, you may want to consider selling your services as an employee to a company that makes software programs. If they need someone to design their software for them, you could work for this company and do just that. If you charge $50 an hour, because that is what the market will bear, then the owner of the company would pay you $10,000 to design his/her program. Now that would be a great start-up business idea! It would also be a great way for someone to get into the business world who doesn't have any money but has lots of computer skills.

Once you've determined what it is that you want to sell and where your customer will buy it, then it's time to think about how much money they are going to pay for your product or service. This is where your research skills come into play. You need to research the market and see how much money people are currently spending on similar products or services to determine what price range people are willing to spend. Sometimes people will pay more for something if they feel like they are getting better quality than if they buy something cheaper but with fewer features. People may also spend more money if they feel as though they are getting a better deal. If you can convince your customer that they are getting a good deal, then they might be willing to pay more than if you don't give them the same feeling.

It is not enough to just sell your product or service at one price and expect it to sell, because there may be too few people who will want to buy your product at that price. You need to find out what the market will bear, or how much you can charge customers for the product or service before too few people are willing to buy it at that price. If no one is willing to buy your product, then you'll have a hard time making money from it.

You should also try to figure out how many people would be interested in buying your product or service. If there aren't enough people who would want your product, then it may not be worth opening a store. Even if you have good marketing skills and can convince everyone who walks into the store that they need what you're selling, if only ten percent of them want it, then you won't make very much money!

The next step in planning your business would be figuring out what kind of store or office space you want to use for selling your product or service. Do you want to rent retail space in a strip mall, or would you rather have an office in the middle of town that can be seen by everyone driving by? You need to evaluate all of these options and figure out which one is best considering the amount of money you want to spend on your business.

We will talk about selecting a location in the next section!

Select a Location

The next step you need to take is selecting a location for your business. There are several things to consider when doing this. You can start your business from home, but you'll want to make sure that it's in a home office and not a bedroom or living room. In other words, make sure that there's enough space in the home for both you and your customers/employees. You'll also want to make sure that your home is safe, secure, and clean. In addition, make sure that your home has enough natural lighting and fresh air. If you will be doing physical work, you'll want your home to be comfortable for your customers/employees as well as yourself.

If you're planning on opening a retail store or a bakery, you'll want to find a location in an area where there are many people. If you're planning on making deliveries, you'll want to find a location in an area where there are many businesses, so that you can deliver products to them. Be sure to check zoning laws before you select any location for your business because if it doesn't meet zoning laws, they may not let you open your business there. The next step would be getting a business license and other permits from the appropriate department of government. Some places require additional licenses and permits such as the fire department or health department depending on the nature of the business and what kind of items are being sold or prepared in the business.

For example, if you're planning on opening a restaurant or a bakery, you'll need to meet the health department's requirements for sanitary conditions as well as certain other requirements. If you're planning on selling alcohol, you'll need to meet the rules and regulations of the state liquor licensing division. You'll also want to check with the city and county in which your business is located before selecting the location.

Write a Business Plan

If you are going to be starting a small business, you should sit down and write out what you plan to do. This is called a business plan[2]. You may not use all of the information in your plan, but writing down your goals and objectives will help keep you on track as you start your new business. There is a lot of information on how to write a business plan that can be found in libraries and bookstores, so we won't get into it here.

Make sure that you include some sort of financial statement as part of your business plan. This will help you come up with an idea of how much money it will take to get started and how much revenue must be made for the company to stay in business. You should also examine the competition that exists in your industry and see if there is any way that you can do something better or different than they are doing already. This helps set yourself apart from the competition right from the beginning.

The other part of the definition of what a business is is that it provides goods and/or services to customers. This means that you have to think about what your business will be selling. If you are selling a service, such as a doctor or a dentist, there are some important things that you must consider before you open for business.

If you are going to be providing a service, there are some things that the customer is expecting from you. First, they expect to get great service; second, they expect their

---

[2] Adam Hayes (updated March 21st 2021) available from https://www.investopedia.com/terms/b/business-plan.asp

problem to be solved; third, they expect their problem to be solved at a reasonable price. You must provide these things for your customers to be happy with their experience with your company.

When people go into an office or the office of a doctor or dentist and sit down in the waiting room, they want to know how long it will take before they see the doctor or dentist. If it is taking too long, then you may lose these customers and no longer have repeat business from them! You must hire extra staff ahead of time so that when the new patient arrives everyone is ready for them and can take care of the patient as quickly as possible. Also, you must make sure that your staff is polite and courteous. If a customer walks in the door, they should be treated as a special customer and made to feel welcome.

If you are going to be selling a product, your business needs to have some sort of unique selling feature that will set it apart from the competition. This feature is called a USP or unique selling proposition. Let's use an example company called "Computer World." This company sells computers and computer-related goods and services to people who want to purchase computer hardware or software products. If this company was going to get repeat business from its customers, then it would need to have some sort of USP that would set it apart from the other computer stores in town.

One way for the company to do this is to create a newsletter[3] for its customers. Every week or so, this newsletter

---

[3] Email marketing (updated July 24th 2020) available from https://blog.e-goi.com/what-is-a-newsletter/

would come out and tell everyone what new products had been added to their inventory and how much money they would save on purchasing those products compared to other stores in town. The newsletter would also contain information about new software programs that had been added or how much money people could save on software updates when they purchased them from Computer World rather than other shops in town.

The newsletter could also contain information about how to use their new software programs. This would help the customers feel good about their purchase and feel confident that they could use the product for a wide range of purposes. Also, they would know that when they go into Computer World, they are getting great service and great deals on all of their products.

We will go through the steps for writing a business plan in detail in the next chapter.

Incorporate Your Business

Many people start small with a business, such as a lawn mowing service or a house cleaning service. Some of these people later decide to expand their business, hire employees and go into office space or other larger facilities. At this point, it becomes much more complicated if the owner is not properly registered with the government. You must get your business registered so that you are legally allowed to do business in your state.

When you register your business name, you will receive an official document called articles of incorporation[4] that puts everything in writing and allows you to legally register as a corporation in the state where you live. You will also be able to purchase insurance for your company and get legal help when needed. You must register your company as soon as possible; time limits vary from state to state, but it is always better to get this done before you need it!

Incorporating your business is also one of the first steps you should take when starting a business. It will make it much easier for you to do business in the future and will help you get out of legal trouble if someone should sue you later on. If you are planning on expanding your business, it is even more important that you incorporate now so that you have all of the necessary paperwork to do so!

There are many different types of business legal structures that you can choose from when you start your business. These structures include sole proprietorship, partnership, limited partnership, limited liability company, and corporation.

Sole Proprietorship

A sole proprietor is someone who owns their business by themselves. For example, if you are a plumber and your name is on the door of your business, then you are a sole

---

[4] Will Kenton (updated October 25th 2020) available from https://www.investopedia.com/terms/a/articlesofincorporation.as p

proprietor. Usually, you will have an LLC[5] or a corporation to protect yourself as the owner—that way, if someone sues you, they can only take your assets and not the property of the company.

The main benefit of a sole proprietorship is simplicity. You don't have to worry about filing additional taxes, and everything stays with the owner. The main disadvantage is that there is no separation between the person and the business, so it could be difficult to expand your business into other locations or hire employees when needed!

Partnerships

A partnership is similar to a sole proprietorship, but there are two or more owners in the company; instead of one person owning it all, each owner has their share in the company. In a partnership, all of the partners have equal say in what happens with money coming in and going out of the company, so everyone has to agree when making decisions. This means that if one partner wants to hire someone else to help run the business, they must get approval from all of the partners before they can make the hire!

Partnerships are a way for two or more people to work together on a project and split the profits. For example, if you have someone great at marketing your business and someone else who is great at running it, then you can create a partnership to help each person do what they do best. You should consider what happens if one of the partners quits

---

[5] Jason Fernando (updated February 28th 2021) available from https://www.investopedia.com/terms/l/llc.asp

before you start your business, so that there are no surprises when it comes time for them to leave!

Limited Partnerships

A limited partnership[6] is like a partnership in that there are two or more owners, and they share in the profits. In this case, however, all of the partners do not have equal say in what happens with money coming in and going out of the company. Usually, there is one general partner who runs the company day-to-day, and there are several limited partners who take advantage of their investment by getting some cash back out but not having as big of an effect on how things work daily. If one of these limited partners decides to quit or passes away, then he/she can be replaced by another person without disrupting how things work—usually!

Limited Liability Companies

A limited liability company, or LLC, is a structure that is becoming more and more popular in the business world. It is a combination of a corporation and a partnership. It has the legal protections of a corporation but the flexibility of a partnership. The owners are called members instead of partners, and they have equal say in how things get done within the company. They also split up the profits equally when it comes time to divide them up.

The main disadvantage of an LLC is that it requires you to file taxes as if it were an S Corporation (an S

---

[6] Evan Tarver (updated March 8th 2021) available from
https://www.investopedia.com/terms/l/limitedpartnership.asp

Corporation does not pay corporate income tax). There are some benefits to this, however, such as being able to deduct business expenses right away rather than waiting until you file your taxes like you would if you were incorporated.

Corporations

A corporation is considered one of the most complex legal structures for businesses. This complexity comes from having to pay income tax on any money coming into or going out of the company at all times during the year. If there are any profits left over at the end of the year, then they need to be distributed to shareholders, and they will receive dividends based upon how much money they have invested in the company. For example, if you were to start a corporation and you owned 60% of the company, you would receive 60% of any profits at the end of the year. You will need to file taxes as if you were an S Corporation[7], which would mean that no taxes would be due until after the company was closed out at the end of the year.

When starting a business, you must decide whether your business should be a sole proprietorship, partnership, limited partnership, limited liability company or corporation. This will depend on how complex your business is and how comfortable you are with filing taxes and dealing with all of the paperwork that goes with it. If your business is going to be simple, and you are not planning on hiring anyone else or expanding outside of your home, then a sole proprietorship could work well for you!

---

[7] Julia Kagan (updated May 25th 2020) available from https://www.investopedia.com/terms/s/subchapters.asp

Register Your Trade Name

Another very important part of starting a company is registering with the government to be able to use your trade name. This is usually done with the state's secretary or department of commerce where you live. In many states, this registration process costs around $10-50[8] per year, which is not too bad when compared to other registration fees. This process can take some time and may require some paperwork, depending on what type of name you plan on using for your company. Sometimes it can be as simple as filling out a form and mailing it in; sometimes it can require that a person go down to their county courthouse and complete paperwork there. You will need to check with your local government office for exact details of how this particular step in starting a company works in your state.

Register for Your Federal Tax ID Number

A federal tax ID number[9] is not as important as the trade name registration, but it is still very important. You will need to register for this number to be able to write a proper business check. This cannot be done until you have received your federal ID number, and it can take some time to receive the number, so it is best to register for it as soon as possible. This particular registration process usually involves going

---

[8] Mary Jane Freeman (updated March 30th 2020) available from https://bizfluent.com/about-5243695-much-cost-register-company-name-.html

[9] IRS, available from https://www.irs.gov/individuals/international-taxpayers/taxpayer-identification-numbers-tin

down to the IRS office in your area and filling out a very short form. It is free and should only take a few minutes of your time, and then you will have a federal tax ID number for your company. Again, you will need to check with your local government office for details on how the process works in your state.

Filing Taxes on Your Company

The last part of starting a company that we will cover here is the filing of taxes on your business. When you begin working with people or making money by selling products or services, you are required by law to pay taxes on these earnings each year. You may be required by law to pay quarterly or monthly depending on how much money you make from doing business. The amount of taxes that you will pay each year is based on how much money you make. The more money that you make means the more taxes you will pay. You can find out what the tax rates are for your state and the federal government by going online to www.irs.gov[10] and looking at their website.

The amount of taxes that you will pay depends on how much money you made during the previous year from your business or other income sources such as a salary from a job. The amount of money it costs to run your company is also factored in when figuring out how much tax you will have to pay on your company's earnings.

---

[10] IRS Filing, https://www.irs.gov/filing

There are several ways to finance your business. The first is by using your own money, either from savings or from a line of credit at the bank. This is one of the most common methods that most new businesses use to start their company.

Another method is to find investors[11] who will pay you for a percentage of the company in exchange for their money. This can be an excellent way to finance your company if you have a good idea and some startup funding. There are also Small Business Administration loan programs that can help you build your business, but they usually provide only enough money to get started; then you must rely on repeat sales for the rest of your financial needs.

The other way that many businesses get financing is by getting some kind of lending or credit agreement with customers before they even open their doors. This sounds impossible because how can you sell something before you even have it? This is another reason why planning is so important! You have to make sure that when your doors finally open, everything will be ready to go for customers, and that there will be enough interest in what you are selling to keep them coming back for more.

You can also consider bootstrapping your business, which means that you start the company without any outside funding at all. This means that you will be doing everything

---

[11] James Chen (updated February 1st 2021) available from https://www.investopedia.com/terms/i/investor.asp

yourself, from selling and marketing your product or service to doing all the bookkeeping and accounting. You may also have to take on some of the sales and marketing tasks as well if your business is particularly small.

Another thing to consider is that many businesses go through several funding cycles before they are finally successful. For example, a business owner may start with his/her own money and prove the business can sell its products or services to customers by getting repeat business. The owners then try to find investors who will invest in their company so they can expand it more quickly. Once those expansions are complete, the owners may try another round of funding from a bank or other lender to expand even more rapidly or to buy out their investors so they can truly control their own company.

This doesn't mean that you should plan on having several rounds of funding, but it might happen if you are very successful with your original idea. Make sure that you have some clear goals for each round of investing as well as a plan for getting there!

Advertise Your Business

Now that you've decided to start your own business, the next thing you need to do is advertise. In the old days, when there were no TVs, no radios, and no internet, it was pretty hard for a new business to get started. It was expensive to print up flyers and newspapers and stuff them in mailboxes. And where would you put these flyers? Local stores wouldn't let you hang them in their windows because they needed those windows for their own advertising! And what about the local radio or TV? These were not options at first, either!

There are several ways that you can advertise your business. The best way to advertise your business is to target your market. If you are marketing to teens, then advertise in places where teens will see your ad. If you have an auto repair shop, then be sure to advertise in the local auto repair shop or car magazines.

The other thing you want to do is make sure that when you create your ad it has a catchy image and is attention-grabbing. You don't want the ad to be too long or too boring—this will get lost in the shuffle among all of the other ads being sent out there. Make it short and sweet, and make sure that it gets people's attention! You can go to Facebook advertising[12] for more information about how this works.

Today we have much better ways of advertising our products and services. The internet has made this possible. There are many different ways of advertising your business over the internet, but here are a few things that you should consider.

Your website should be professionally designed and built. If you have a good website, then people will find you on the internet and will be able to use it to find your contact information. You should also think about how your website can be used as a platform to sell your products and services.

---

[12] Facebook for business,
https://www.facebook.com/business/ads

This is called e-commerce—where you sell something over the internet.

You should consider using social media sites like Facebook or Twitter to advertise your business. These sites are very popular with people who want to share what they have been doing or what they are doing tomorrow...the next day...or even months from now! If you can get people interested in your business, it will be easy for them to find out about it and share it with their friends.

You should also consider advertising with local newspapers, local radio stations, and other local sources. People still read newspapers and listen to the radio, so advertising in both of these media sources can be very effective. It's important that if you choose one of these media sources, it has a wide enough audience that includes the people you are trying to attract as customers.

Consider having some sort of flyer or brochure printed up for potential customers that they can take home with them after they meet with you face-to-face. This can help you get their contact information so you can follow up with them later.

All of these forms of advertising will help you attract customers to your business.

Chapter 2: Business Plan – The Key to Successful Business Planning

The first step in creating your business plan is to identify exactly what you want to do. You should have a clear idea about what you will be offering and who your customers and competitors are. How much money will it take? How much time will it require? What skills will you need? What support systems are essential for success?

Once you have answers to these questions, look at the overall picture. What do these facts tell you about resources, both financial and human, will be required? How can they be obtained? Are there other steps that should be taken before starting this venture? Remember, there is no substitute for careful planning and preparation. Only by knowing exactly where you are going can you determine the best way of getting there.

What is a Business Plan?

A business plan is a written description of how you intend to make your business a success. A business plan forces you to clarify your goals, anticipate problems, and recognize the resources that will be needed to achieve success. It is a blueprint for action.

Business Plan Outline: An Overview

A good business plan is a roadmap that shows how a new business or venture will succeed. It should include all the elements of a successful business, including marketing strategy, financials (including projected profit and loss statements), and management team information. A good business plan includes goals, objectives, and strategies to achieve those goals. A business plan is often accompanied by a feasibility study that looks at the market potential of an idea or product. The study provides an analysis of the strengths and weaknesses of a project's proposed approach to solving customer problems or needs while maintaining a competitive advantage against other products or services in the marketplace.

A business plan is the formal statement of goals, strategies, and objectives for a new business or venture within an existing business. In addition to financial projections, a business plan should include descriptions of the management team and their qualifications, detailed marketing plans and sales forecasts, as well as legal issues related to the launch of the company. A good business plan will also include recommendations for funding sources and key personnel.

The purpose of a business plan is to serve as a road map that helps guide entrepreneurs in achieving their goals. A good business plan will communicate that vision to an investor, banker, or other interested parties who can help make that vision become reality. When you're ready to present your business idea professionally, use our easy-to-use templates to create your own and show investors your commitment to excellence.

What's in a Business Plan?

The business plan must include a description of the business itself and how it will be operated. It should also include a description of the market in which the business will operate and how it will be promoted. Finally, it must include a cash flow forecast and projections of costs and revenues. The following is a list of items that should be included in your plan:

A description of your business including its legal form (sole proprietorship, partnership, corporation), what you will offer to the customer, any special skills or expertise needed to run the venture successfully, the name and address of those who are running the venture (the owner).

A description of your competition: who they are, what they do better than you, what their weaknesses are.

A brief description of any company support services or programs that may be required to run your business. For example, advertising agency or public relations firm; legal counsel (e.g., lawyer or accountant); insurance agent; marketing consultant; sales representative (e.g., sales agent); tax accountant; shipping company or courier service.

An outline of your marketing strategy: Who is your market? What channels are you going to use to reach them? How are you going to convince customers to buy from you instead of your competitors? What will be the special features of your business that will set it apart from the competition?

A description of your product or service. For example, if you are starting a restaurant, what type of food will you serve? How about a bakery? A fitness center? A law practice?

The type and amount of equipment (e.g., computers, inventory, etc.) needed to operate your business. You may want to include an estimate of the total dollar value and where and how it will be obtained (e.g., bank loan, savings, etc.).

How much start-up capital[13] is required to get the venture off the ground (e.g., equipment, inventory, etc.) and how it will be obtained (e.g., savings, loans).

An outline of operating expenses. Include costs such as labor costs (wages or salaries); rent or lease payments for premises (including insurance); telephone and utility services; the advertising budget for promotion and advertising materials (such as brochures, signs, etc.); costs for packaging materials for shipping products or goods out to customers; payroll taxes; legal expenses required to establish the business; travel costs involved in promoting your business; and any other fixed expenses that are related to operating the business.

A list of additional cash requirements. For example, will you need to purchase insurance for your employees or the business property? When will it be needed?

An estimate of revenues: from what sources (e.g., sales or fees); how much you expect to make in the first year, second

---

[13] Carol M. Kopp (updated December 30th 2020) available from https://www.investopedia.com/terms/s/startup-capital.asp

year, third year; and what is needed to keep the venture profitable (e.g., projected sales increases, cost reductions).

A cash flow forecast[14]: an estimate of your cash inflows and outflows for a specified period such as one month or one year. This should include a detailed explanation of each item listed. For example, if you are using savings as a source of start-up capital, explain why savings will not be needed later on (e.g., profits).

How much profit you expect to make in each month or year; how this profit will be used (e.g., expansion, paying off debt); whether any money is needed for savings; whether additional equity capital is required to sustain the venture; what new ventures can be financed with the profits generated by the original venture if there is excess cash.

A list of factors and events that could affect the business and must be considered when planning how to run the business. For example, if you are operating a retail store, what would happen if a nearby retail store closed or was sold? What would this do to your business? What if there is a recession and your customers have no money? What other businesses are competing with yours for advertising dollars? Is there anything else that could affect your success or failure in operating the business?

A list of resources available to support the venture: government agencies, trade associations, private organizations, etc.

---

[14] Martin Gillespie, https://www.cashanalytics.com/what-is-cash-flow-forecasting/

These are only a few items that should be included in your business plan. Many other possibilities could be a factor depending on the kind of business you are starting. If you are starting a new venture, the first place to look for information is the Small Business Administration[15] (SBA) and local government agencies. These organizations have experts who can help you identify the resources that will be needed to get a venture off the ground.

How to Write a Business Plan?

There are many parts to a business plan, but all of them relate to the following information:

Company Description

Make a list of the skills you have and those that you will need to obtain to succeed in your field. What do you know about your company's strengths and weaknesses? What are its marketable assets? How will it be positioned in the marketplace? Are there any potential problems that could threaten the success of your business venture?

---

[15] SBA, https://www.sba.gov/

Product or Service Description

Think of your product or service as if it were a person. What is his/her name? Why are you interested in him/her? How do you plan to get to know him/her better? What characteristics does he/she have (e.g., personality, age, appearance, education level)? Is he/she trustworthy, reliable, loyal, and stable? Will he/she be an asset or a liability to your company? The more information you can gather about this "person," the better idea you will have of what kind of support systems are needed for him or her to succeed.

Market Analysis

<u>Who is Going to Buy Your Product or Service?</u>

- List each group who might purchase your product or service and describe them in detail (age, gender, etc.). For each group, list the reasons why they would or would not buy your product or service.
- What is the size of the market? How many potential customers are there in your community, state, region, or country?
- What is the potential growth of this market? How many new customers will you add each year? Where will they come from (new people moving into your area, a change in a competitor's business, etc.)?
- Who are your competitors[16] and how do you differ from them? Do they offer quality products at competitive prices? What special services do they offer

---

[16] Competitor, https://marketbusinessnews.com/financial-glossary/competitor-definition-meaning/

that you can't match? What can you offer that no one else can match? Are you going to be able to maintain a competitive edge over them in the future? Are there any potential threats to your position in this market (a new technology that may make this product obsolete)?

Management Plan

Who Will Run Your Business, and How Will It Be Organized for Maximum Effectiveness and Efficiency? Describe each person who will be involved in running the business and describe their specific roles and responsibilities. Make a list of all equipment that is necessary for running your business. In what order will these items be purchased? Do you need to hire someone to do any of the jobs that will need to be done? If so, what skills will they need, and how much will it cost you?

Marketing Plan

How Will You Attract Potential Customers and Establish a Profitable Business? What are the strengths and weaknesses of your product or service? What factors will make your product or service attractive or unattractive in the marketplace? How does this product or service fit into the larger market picture? How does your product or service differ from those of your competitors? Who is going to be responsible for developing and implementing this plan, and what resources (money, people, equipment) are needed for success?

Operations Plan

What Will Your Company Do to Make Money? List all of the products or services that you plan to offer. Describe each one in detail. How is each item different from its competition, and how can it be made more attractive than its competition through price, quality, variety, etc.? What are your company's strengths and weaknesses concerning these products/services? What factors make it easier or harder for you to make money with these products/services (e.g., market size, competitor's positions in that market, etc.)?

Financial Plan

How Much Money Will You Need to Run Your Business, and How Will You Get It? Make a list of the money that you will need to operate your business (e.g., equipment, supplies, insurance, sales and marketing costs, rent). List all of the people who will be involved in this aspect of the business (salespeople, bookkeepers, accountants, delivery people, etc.). How much money is each person going to need, and how much time will they need from you to do their jobs properly? What steps can you take now to raise the money that you will need later (e.g., savings accounts, loans from family and friends)? What steps must be taken before you can start making money? When do you expect to be profitable? Do you plan on hiring someone else at some point in the future if your business becomes more profitable than it is now?

Personnel Plan

What Are You Going to Pay Yourself and Why? Determine what salary should be paid to yourself based on what other people are making in similar businesses or based on what your expenses are. If other employees are going to work for your company at any time during its existence, determine how much their salary should be based on the following: (a) what they will bring to the business (skills, experience, etc.), (b) what you can afford to pay them, and (c) what is fair concerning similar businesses.

Miscellaneous Plan

What Else is Needed to Make Your Business a Success? List all of the other things that you will need for your business to succeed (e.g., signs, brochures, letterhead, business cards). These items are not as important as people or money, but they must be considered. What steps will you take now to obtain these items later?

How to Make the Plan Work for You?

Two essential elements will help make your business plan work for you:

The first element is a "must-have"—a clear, step-by-step plan of action that you can follow to achieve your goal. This means writing down and listing exactly what you intend to do, how long it will take to do it, and how much money will be required. It also means your business plan must be realistic. It must not only reflect the capabilities of yourself and any partners but also the resources available to you. Make sure that everything in your plan is achievable and that nothing in it is so unrealistic as to make achieving your goals impossible. Remember, if you fail to achieve those goals, there is little chance of success for your business.

The second essential element for success is an understanding of the importance of planning on each level. In other words, if you want to succeed in running a successful business, then you must learn to plan at every level—from planning for a summer vacation adventure with the family or friends, through planning your workday as a salesclerk or office worker, through planning an advertising campaign for a major corporation—because planning works at all levels! Planning can't guarantee success, but it can help you to achieve success by making your business more effective and more profitable.

What Are the Best Ways to Write Your Business Plan?

There are a few best ways that you can present your plan. Here are ten tips for you when creating your business plan.

Keep it simple

The best way to write your business plan is on a single sheet of paper. Do not try to include everything you want to say in one big document. If you do, you will probably bog down in details and never get started.

Write about your business and your customers, not about yourself

Your business plan should serve as a guide for getting things done, not as a vehicle for telling people about yourself or extolling your virtues. It should be about the business and its objectives: what it is going to do, how you are going to make it work, why it will succeed, what customers you expect to serve, what competition exists, how you plan to overcome that competition and other necessary items related to the venture.

Include only those facts that are necessary for the presentation of your idea

The purpose of the business plan is to identify opportunities and develop strategies for exploiting them successfully. You should be concerned with planning goals that can be achieved with defined resources available at zero or minimal cost. Excessive detail may be another way of saying "I have no idea where I am going." A detailed outline of every step needed from start-up through final liquidation may be nothing more than an admission that you have no idea how to succeed.

Write in the present tense

Write as though you are actually involved in the business and have already accomplished all you set out to do. Use the present tense, not the future tense. Thus, a statement such as "We will build a better mousetrap" is fine; a statement like "We will build a better mousetrap when we start operations" is not fine because it indicates that this is still just a dream and has not become reality.

Be positive and optimistic, but realistic

A business plan should be positive and optimistic about its chances for success—but realistic as well. Do not get carried away with your enthusiasm, or there is sure to be disappointment later on when reality sets in. A good rule of thumb: if what you are writing sounds too good to be true, it probably isn't true!

Avoid jargon and complexity whenever possible

If you can state your message clearly, do so—especially if you are trying to reach a wide audience (employees, suppliers, banks, or others who may want to know more about your operation), but don't try to impress people with big words or complex jargon.

Use graphic aids to clarify your points

A picture is worth a thousand words, so use charts or graphs to illustrate your ideas. Charts and graphs are very effective when used with simple language and straightforward explanations.

Provide plenty of white space to help the reader skim easily through your business plan

Don't be afraid to use white space on the page—it can make a big difference in how easy it is to read your business plan, as well as how attractive the finished product looks. The best business plans are concise, not crowded. It may be hard at first for you to keep from writing too much, but try to hold back until you have said all you need to say in the least number of words possible. You will find that this is one of the real keys to good writing: say everything concisely in such a way that the reader benefits from reading it without getting bored or bogged down by lengthy explanations or examples that don't add anything. When you think about it, this is one of the most difficult things an author can do—yet, it's also one of the most important.

Use action words and positive statements

Avoid negative or passive phrases such as "To avoid problems, we will not do..." Instead use positive statements, such as "We will..." or "We plan to..." This is a good way to keep your business plan from becoming a litany of "I will nots..." Keep in mind that the purpose of the business plan is to help you achieve your goals, not to tell what you can't do.

Don't be afraid to change your business plan when necessary

You can always revise your business plan later on if necessary, but if you never do anything because you are just waiting for things to change before you start, all you'll accomplish is changing from one dream into another. Remember that writing a good business plan is like putting together a jigsaw puzzle—all the pieces have to fit together just right for the answer to emerge clearly. A good business plan helps you make sure all those pieces are in place so that when it's time for action, the most important thing is getting started right away!

What About Financial Forecasts?

Be sure to include a financial forecast[17] in your business plan. This is the most important part of your business plan and will help you determine if the venture is worth pursuing.

The first step in creating a financial forecast is to make a list of all the expenses you will incur in starting and running your business each year. Include everything, from the cost of renting or purchasing property or equipment, to wages and salaries for employees, insurance premiums, telephone charges, postage costs, advertising costs, travel expenses and any other costs that you can think of. Be sure to include all start-up expenses as well as continuing operating expenses.

An excellent rule of thumb for start-up expenses is to expect that they will be at least 20% of annual sales revenues. For example, if you hope to make $50,000 during the first year of operation, you should expect to spend at least $10,000 just on startup costs (rental space, etc.). This may sound like a lot, but consider that most businesses spend at least 20% on sales promotion during their first year, so it isn't that much more than what is normally spent.

---

[17] Financial forecasting, https://www.toolshero.com/financial-management/financial-forecasting

Once you have completed your list, add up all the figures for start-up and annual operating expenses and divide them by the number of days in a year (365 in the example below). If your annual expenses equal $5,000 and there are 365 days in a year, then you need to earn $13.69 per day to pay all expenses and have enough left over for your family's living expenses.

Example: Assume that the annual expense figure is $5,000.00 and there are 365 days in a year. This means that your business must generate approximately $13.69 per day to at least break-even[18].

If you decide that this is too high an amount to make a profit on only one sale per day, consider lowering some of the fixed costs, or increasing revenues by adding additional products or services to your product line, or raising prices. Don't be afraid to do this because customers will not mind paying more for higher, quality goods or better service so long as they get what they want in return for their money. However, you should still do everything possible to keep your start-up costs down by using things like home offices, second-hand office furniture or buying used computers and typewriters. Remember, no matter how much money you spend on start-up costs, the important thing is that you can show you have thought the plan through carefully and are willing to put your own money into the business to make it a success.

---

[18] Break-even, https://en.wikipedia.org/wiki/Break-even

Chapter 3: Bootstrapping a Business – Lean Startup, No Capital Needed

The world is filled with people that have a great idea for a product or service, but it's the execution that matters. On this page, we'll discuss how to start your own business with limited startup capital.

The first thing you need to do is define your idea. What do you want to build? Think about the best way to solve the problem and get it out there so people can use it. Once you have an idea, you need to get started on building your product or service. This is where bootstrapping[19] comes in—limited money required! How can you get this off the ground? Let's dive right in.

The Lean Startup Method

The Lean Startup Method is a great way to get started on your idea without the need for outside capital. It's an approach to building a business by focusing on discovering the "right" product or service to build by validating your ideas with customers and learning from those interactions.

---

[19] Will Kenton (updated September 20th 2020) available from https://www.investopedia.com/terms/b/bootstrap.asp.

The Lean Startup Method was developed by Eric Ries[20], a Silicon Valley[21] entrepreneur who spent over a decade working for startups. He's the author of *The Lean Startup*[22], which has sold over one million copies worldwide.

Here are the three steps you need to follow:

Build Your Minimum Viable Product (MVP)

This is the first step in any business—you've got to create something that people want. The "Minimum Viable Product" is exactly that—your minimum viable product. It's what you need to get started, nothing more and nothing less. You're not going to build everything at this point, just enough that you can start validating your idea with customers and learning how they use your product or service. This helps you get feedback early on so that you can see if there's a market for what you're doing before investing too much time and energy into building something nobody wants. Think about it this way—if you build something nobody wants, you're going to have a very difficult time getting customers. You need to find out if anyone wants your product or service before spending too much time on your idea.

[20] Eric Ries, https://en.wikipedia.org/wiki/Eric_Ries
[21] Troy Segal (updated October 27th 2020) available from https://www.investopedia.com/terms/s/siliconvalley.asp.
[22] The lean start-up, https://en.wikipedia.org/wiki/The_Lean_Startup

Now that you've got something to show people, it's time to get feedback! This is where the Lean Startup Method differs from other methods on how to start a business. If you're building an app, you don't need to spend millions of dollars on advertising—you just need someone willing to try it out and give feedback. The goal is to cut out the middleman and get direct customer feedback without spending any money on marketing or advertising. This allows us to focus more on the product or service we're creating and less on raising money first. The goal is to find out if anyone wants what you're offering them before spending too much time building something nobody wants.

Learn from Your Customers

In this step, it's all about learning from your customers what they want for them to use your product or service more! How can we improve? What can we do differently? What changes should we make? We are focused back on the product or service that we're building by learning from customer feedback. This is a great way to start your own business without spending a lot of money upfront.

Launching Your Business

Bootstrapping a business is all about getting started and learning how to run a business on the cheap. It's about validating your idea before you spend huge amounts of time and money on developing it further. Let's dive into how to get started with bootstrapping a business and saving some cash along the way!

There's No Need to Raise Capital

When we're bootstrapping a business, we're not going to spend money on marketing or advertising. Instead, we'll focus on building a product or service that people want. This means that if you're building an app, you don't need to spend a million dollars on marketing before getting started. Instead, you just need someone willing to try it out and give feedback.

The goal is to get feedback on the product or service you're creating without spending any money on marketing or advertising. The idea is to get early validation from customers so that you can learn if anyone wants what you're offering them before spending too much time building something nobody wants!

Focus on Your Idea Instead of Making It Look Pretty

When bootstrapping a business, there's no need to worry about how your product or service looks—just focus on the actual functionality and getting it out there so people can use it! The Lean Startup Method focuses more on functionality than how pretty your User Interface[23] looks. It's all about solving problems for your customers and helping them solve their problems with whatever solution you come up with. The success of your business is dependent upon solving problems for people. How are they going to use your product or service?

---

[23] User interface, https://techterms.com/definition/user_interface

What are they going to do with it? How can it help them solve their problems?

Keep It Simple

Don't worry about building everything you want at first. Start with the minimum viable product—just what you need to get started. You'll have the chance to evolve your product as you learn from customers, but don't go overboard at first. Instead, focus on building something that solves a real problem for people. How can you help them solve their problems? You're trying to solve a problem that people have and get paid for it. This is a great way to start your own business without spending too much money upfront on development!

Get Feedback from Customers

There's no need to wait for feedback from customers after developing the product or service—the goal is to get some initial feedback before developing anything further. This is where the Lean Startup Method differs from other methods on how to start a business. If you're building an app, you don't need to spend millions of dollars on advertising—instead, focus on getting feedback directly from customers and learning what will make them want to use your product or service more. Once you've validated your idea, it's time to start building the real product or service!

Learn how to start your own business on the cheap and save some cash while learning what you need to know about the business. This is a great way to learn how to run a successful business using limited capital. You won't need millions of dollars to get started. Just get started with the right mindset, and learn what you can from customers.

The Lean Canvas - A Visual Storyboard for the Lean Startup Method

The Lean Startup Method[24] is a new way to build products and services. This method involves creating a storyboard called the Lean Canvas. This canvas will help you visualize your startup ideas and get feedback from potential customers. You need to create a storyboard so you can visualize how people will use your product or service and what their needs are that you'll be able to support. This will help you to determine if your idea is a good one.

The Lean Canvas[25] is an easy way for you to get started with a startup business. It's like a storyboard that provides visuals for you to understand the idea of your business and how it will work.

How does this work? Once you create your Lean Canvas, put it up on the wall where everyone can see it. Then ask people to fill out their ideas or give feedback about what they see on the canvas. Do they think this product or service is something they would use? Are they interested in it? What can be changed to make them more interested? You'll want to

---

[24] Lean start-up methods, http://theleanstartup.com/principles
[25] Lean canvas, https://leanstack.com/lean-canvas

invite everyone who might be interested in your product or service, especially ones who have expertise in the field. The more people who give you feedback, the more accurate your storyboard becomes and allows for better decision-making moving forward.

At first, your idea might seem like a great one, but once people provide feedback, you'll begin to understand how other people feel about it and why they are or are not interested in your product or service. This could mean that you need to change something about the idea so that it appeals more to people, or it could mean that you'll need to change some things about your product or service before you launch it.

The Lean Canvas is a visual storyboard that will help you to get feedback and create a better product or service for the people who will be using it.

Here is what you need to know about this tool:

- It's a visual tool that will help you to get feedback from potential customers. You can share it with anyone who has expertise in your industry or who might be interested in the product or service and ask for feedback. This allows you to find out what people think about your idea and why they like or dislike it.
- It will help you to visualize how people will use your product or service before you invest any money into creating it. This is important so that your idea has a chance at success. By visualizing how people will use the product, you'll have a better idea of what's important to them and how they'd like to use it. By

understanding this, you'll be able to determine if your concept is worth investing money into creating the product or service.

- It allows you to see what parts of the business are more important than others. For example, if the customer experience is more important than the revenue-generating capabilities of your product or service, then this is an important factor that should be highlighted on your canvas. Knowing what's most important helps you to make decisions about how you should move forward with your startup idea.

- The Lean Canvas gives people a visual to understand how the product or service will work. The storyboard helps you to visualize how people will use it and what their needs are, which gives you a better understanding of how your product or service will be received.

- By getting feedback from multiple people, you'll be able to get a better understanding of your idea and how people will feel about it. You'll learn what works and what doesn't by getting feedback from others. This allows you to visualize the strengths and weaknesses of your idea, which helps you make better decisions moving forward.

- The Lean Canvas allows for an easy way to visualize the customer experience with the product or service that you're creating. It allows for an easy way to help you understand what's important in terms of usability so that your customers can use it easily. If it's difficult to use, then this is something that should be highlighted on your canvas so you can make changes before creating it.

- The Lean Canvas is a great tool for helping start-ups visualize their ideas, which gives them a better understanding of what works best in their business model before they invest any money into creating the product or service.

Here are the various parts of the Lean Canvas:

Problem

What is the problem that your product or service will help to solve? Why will people buy it? How big is the market for your idea? This part of your storyboard is like the driver behind the product or service. It's what's making you want to build it and get it out there, but why do people need it?

Solution

How does your product or service solve that problem? What needs does it meet that clients have? People are going to want to know exactly how you're going to help them solve this problem. This is what makes them interested in using your product or service, which determines if they buy it or not.

Unique Value Proposition

What makes you different from everyone else? Just because you have a great idea doesn't mean you'll be successful at getting people interested in it and buying it from you. If everyone else is selling products that do what yours does, then how are they different from each other? What makes yours stand out from the rest of them, and why should buyers choose yours over someone else's? If you can't answer these questions clearly, then chances are people won't buy from you.

Customer Segments

Who is going to be interested in your product or service? Who is going to buy it? What are they looking for? Knowing who your target customer base will be will help you to better understand what they need and why they'll choose your product or service over someone else's offering. This will also help you to better target your advertising and how you market this to them.

Key Activities

How do people accomplish this task? What do they need to do and know to get the work done? If you're going to sell your product or service, what does the buyer need to know for them to use it and feel like it worked for them? How can you make a process that's as easy as possible for them, so that they can have the best experience using it? The easier it is for them, the more likely it is that they'll say yes when someone asks if they would recommend your product or service over another one.

Key Resources

What resources do people need for this process to work? What skills do customers need or have so that things run smoothly with their purchase? What equipment do they need for this to work? If you're selling a product, what do they need to know how to do for it to work?

Key Partners

Who else are people going to need help from for this process to work? What else will they need so that your product or service continues to run without any problems?

Revenue Streams

How are you going to get paid? What do you need for your product or service to be profitable? Are you going to charge per copy or by how many times it's used? Will people pay a one-time fee or an annual subscription? How will you know that your customers will continue using it so that it continues making money for you and keeps the business running without any problems (or at least as few as possible)?

Cost Structure

How much is everything going to cost for you and the customer when using this product or service? This includes everything from getting started, how much it costs them each time they use the product or service and what expenses are needed each time they use it. How much will all of these things cost, and what does the customer need to know about that?

Customer Relationships

How do people interact with the product or service? What kind of relationship does the customer have with this product or service and how do they feel about it? You'll need to know how they feel about your product or service and why they would choose it over someone else's. They will need to like it and want others to know that they use it.

Channels

How do you get the word out there about your product or service? What are you going to tell people about it so that they'll be interested in using it if their problem is something your product or service can solve? Will you go door-to-door, create a website, or post on social media? How are you going to let people know this product or service exists? Will you advertise in magazines, on TV or online? Where will you place ads so that people can find out about your new business and what it has to offer them? You'll want as many people as possible to hear about what you have to offer because once they know about it, they just might buy from you.

Validation - The First Step of the Lean Startup Method

One thing you can do as part of the Lean Startup Method is validate your product before you invest in it. Validation is a good approach because you can learn about your market without spending too much money. It's also a great way to start a business without capital because you'll be investing in more tests rather than just one product or service.

What is Validation?

It's how you learn about your market and how to solve the problem. It's testing the idea. There are many ways to validate your idea, but here are some of the most common ones:

Talking to People

This means you go out and talk with potential customers or people that may be interested in your product or service. Don't sell anything; just ask them what they think and what they need. You'll probably get some great feedback that will help you narrow down the idea or create a new one based on their needs.

Google It

You can use a search engine[26] to find out how many people are looking for the same information you provide with your idea. This is great for finding out how popular your idea is and how much of a need there is for it.

Email It

This is the same as talking to people, but you can do it from home! It's a great way to reach out to potential customers and start building your email list. If you're starting a blog, it's even better because you'll have an audience right away.

Build a Prototype

---

[26] Search engine, https://en.wikipedia.org/wiki/Search_engine

You can either go out and build the real product or service or create a mock-up of it. Either way, if you build something, people will see what you're doing and be more likely to buy-in. On a business-related note, you'll also learn more about how the market works.

Get Feedback

This one is great because it gives insight into how people think about your product or service. You can do this by sending out surveys, asking for comments on social media, and getting feedback from friends and family members.

Keep in mind that there are many other ways to validate your idea as well! The main thing is to get started with getting feedback before investing too much time and money into building something that no one wants.

Don't Spend Any Money – Use Free Tools and Services Instead

The first thing you need to do is figure out what your product or service will be and how it will work. You can use tools like Google Drive, Dropbox, Trello, and Asana to create a visual roadmap for your project. When you have an idea, you can use simple tools like SurveyMonkey[27] or Typeform[28] to find out what people think about your idea. If needed, you can also use free tools like Dropbox Paper or Google Drive Docs to make it look more professional.

---

[27] SurveyMonkey, https://www.surveymonkey.com/
[28] Typeform, https://www.typeform.com/

There are many different task management software tools out there. Some of the most popular ones are Basecamp, Trello, and Wrike. You should use one of these to help you keep track of all your tasks and projects. You could also use Google Drive Tasks or Asana to keep a running list of things you need to do.

You can also use free tools and services like Wufoo, Mailchimp, HelpScout[29], and Zendesk[30] to create a simple website. Once you have your idea, you can see if people are interested in it with something like SurveyMonkey or Typeform. Don't spend any money on these tools—they're free!

If you don't have the money for a professional domain name, you can get one for free using Google Domains or Hover.com. Domain names generally cost around $2-20[31] per year—so if you can't afford that, use a free option!

Outsourcing Your Product Development – How to Get Things Done on a Shoestring Budget

You can use outsourcing to help build your product for a fraction of the cost. You have a great idea, but don't know how to get it out there. A good rule of thumb is to ask yourself, "Can I do this myself?" If the answer is yes, you may want to consider doing it yourself. This will allow you to learn and understand how your product works so that you can better support it long-term.

---

[29] HelpDesk https://www.helpscout.com/
[30] ZenDesk, https://www.zendesk.com/
[31] Maxym Martineu (updated July 8th 2019) https://www.godaddy.com/garage/how-much-domain-name-cost/

However, if the answer is no, then you need to find someone who can do it for a price that makes sense for your business. Finding a freelancer or contractor is easy enough. You can find them on sites like Upwork or Freelancer[32]. However, finding someone that you can trust with your ideas and getting things done quickly may be difficult if you aren't familiar with the process of hiring a freelancer/contractor and vetting them for their skill set.

If this sounds like something you want to avoid and focus on building rather than hiring people, there are plenty of services online that will do all of this for you. Sites like Fiverr allow you access to thousands of freelancers/contractors from around the world with skillsets ranging from designing logos to writing code. A lot of people are skeptical about services like Fiverr because they often get low quality work. However, it is up to you to set the expectations with the freelancer/contractor and make sure that they are getting the work done for you. Just because you pay a small amount for your product doesn't mean that it's easy to build.

The great thing about outsourcing is that it allows you to focus on what you do best and outsource everything else! When working with a freelancer or contractor, make sure you are clear on exactly what they need to do and how long each task should take. Also, it's best to have more than one person working on your project at any given time so that there is not too much downtime waiting for things to be completed.

---

[32] FreeLancer, https://www.freelancer.com/

If this sounds like something that would work for you, there are some things you need to keep in mind when hiring someone:

Communication – This is the key ingredient in any relationship, whether personal or business-related. If communication breaks down, things fall apart quickly! Set expectations early on as well as deadlines, so there are no surprises later on.

Don't be afraid to ask questions – This is the person you are paying, and they should be doing everything in their power to make sure that you are getting what you need. If something is not clear, ask a question! Don't be afraid to ask for more details and be sure that everything is understood upfront.

Test your product – Once your product is done, see if it works! A lot of freelancers/contractors get paid and never test to make sure things run smoothly. Spending a little extra time on this will help ensure that you won't have to go through revisions once the project is complete.

No one wants to fail or spend money on something that doesn't work. However, it's possible to bootstrap a business with limited capital in today's market. It's going to take some effort on your part, but it could lead you to great success!

Find a Mentor

A mentor[33] is someone who has been in business for a long time and has learned many things from experience. A mentor can give you advice on your business and can show you the ropes so you know what to do in the future.

---

[33] Scott Allen (updated June 18th 2019) https://www.thebalancesmb.com/the-value-of-a-business-mentor-1200818

Here are some ways that a mentor can help you:

- Someone to tell you what to do. You can ask your mentor what you should do in a given situation, and he or she will tell you the best way to handle it.
- If you have a question about how something works, your mentor can explain it to you.
- You can talk with your mentor to see if he or she has any suggestions for improving your business. Your mentor can also help you figure out how to deal with problems that come up from time to time.
- Make sure that the person who wants to be your mentor is someone who understands the kind of business that you run and knows how similar businesses operate. Your mentor should be someone who runs a similar business or has experience in other related businesses.
- Your mentor should know other people who own businesses like yours and may be able to give you contacts for other people in your industry if needed. Your mentor should also know about resources such as financing and advertising that may help run a successful business. Choose someone honest, trustworthy, and fair-minded when choosing a good advisor for your company.
- If your mentor has been successful in his or her own business, then he or she will understand what it takes to succeed. If you have the opportunity to get a mentor, take it! You will be glad that you did.

Find a mentor who is in a business that you would like to be in. A mentor can help you out so much. If your mentor has been in the business for a long time, ask them how they got started in their business and why they are still doing it. They will most likely say they enjoy what they do and that it has been good to them. You'll need to always remember this because it'll let you know that no matter what happens with the business, just keep doing what you're doing, and don't give up.

You could also go to an organization or club and talk with other people who are in the same business as you are or want to be in. You could talk about how things are going for your company and how things are going for theirs, too! It's great when people come together to talk about their businesses because they all get ideas on how to make their companies better. Also, if someone needs any help with their company or if they need some advice, they can ask their friends who are in the same business as them.

If you have a mentor, take notes on what they tell you. If your mentor has been in the business for a long time and you want to be in the business for a long time, then write down important information that you need to know. Don't just write down what your mentor is telling you, but also write down what you think will help your company grow more.

Chapter 4: Marketing Basics – Six Steps to Marketing Success

Marketing[34] is an essential part of running a business. If you don't market your business, it could have no customers and therefore fail. Marketing is the process of promoting your business to your potential customers. The marketer's goal is to create a demand for his product, which increases the likelihood of sales. A good marketing plan is essential for every business to succeed.

In this chapter, we examine the six steps to marketing success.

Begin with a Plan

The first thing you need to start marketing your business successfully is to have a plan. This plan will let you know where you are going and how to get there. It will also show you the steps that are needed. The plan should contain a description of your product or service, who your customers are, what market segment they fall into, which consumers need this product or service the most, what your competition is doing (if any), and how you will beat them at their game.

A good business plan contains all of these things and more. It should also include a marketing strategy and an action

---

[34] Alexandra Twin (updated August 17th 2020)
https://www.investopedia.com/terms/m/marketing.asp

plan with specific objectives for each action item. The action items should be measurable so that success can be determined. For example, your action item might be to create a new advertising campaign. This action item should have a specific objective. Your objective might be that you want to see 1,500 leads in the next six months. If you are selling $2,000,000 worth of product per year, you need to sell about 33 leads per month. That is a reasonable number of leads. Is your advertising campaign going to attract 1,500 leads? Is it going to cost more than $20,000? Are the leads qualified?

The answer to these questions is not known until after the campaign is launched and the results are analyzed. The results can be analyzed by taking calls from prospective customers and qualifying them as either sale-ready[35] or not sale-ready (i.e., not likely to become a customer).

Once you have your business plan in hand and know where you are going with it and how you will get there, the next step is to develop an implementation plan that will get your marketing campaign underway. It will include an analysis of all aspects of marketing such as advertising, public relations[36] (PR), direct mail campaigns, selling strategies, and sales campaigns, including telemarketing approaches and other marketing tools like seminars or trade shows.

[35] Josh Patrick, https://www.stage2planning.com/blog/what-is-a-sale-ready-business
[36] Pranashree S, https://www.economicsdiscussion.net/marketing-management/what-is-public-relations/31834

Your implementation plan should include a timeline for the execution of each action item. It should also include the estimated costs for each action item and how you will get the money to pay for it.

The implementation plan should be specific, measurable, achievable, and realistic. If you think your plan is realistic and achievable, then you are ready to move on to the next step: identifying potential customers.

The marketing plan should also include a description of your target market. What characteristics do they have? How did you determine which consumers need your product the most?

Marketing should not be thought of as an event, but rather as an ongoing process that should be reviewed and updated regularly. This will help you see how well the plan is working and make any necessary adjustments.

Marketing is a complex subject that can't be covered in just one chapter. Therefore, we will concentrate on the basics of marketing that are needed to get you started. We will also cover some of the more popular marketing methods and techniques that are being used today.

Identify Potential Customers

The first step in marketing is to determine who your potential customers[37] are. A business that sells products or services to an existing market doesn't have to do any research. However, if you are trying to create a new market for your product, you must know what customers want.

If you're planning on selling a new type of product or service, try doing some research in your local area to see if there is a demand for it. You may also want to read the newspaper and check out recent trends in the industry. Make sure you ask yourself how many people would actually buy the product or service and how much they would be willing to pay for it.

For example, if you plan on selling a new type of cleaning product, it would be best to find out if there is a demand for it. If many people are interested in your product, then you can go ahead and start marketing. If not, you may want to try a different product or service.

It is important to figure out how much people are willing to pay for your product or service. If you set the price too low, the sales will be low, and it will be hard to cover your costs. If you set the price too high, then there won't be any customers.

---

[37] Potential customers,
https://www.burstcreative.com.au/graphic-design/potential-customers.

The best way to determine how much you should charge for a product or service is by using a pricing method called cost-plus pricing. This involves using your production costs as a base and adding what it will cost to sell and distribute the product. You can also use market research to determine what others are charging for similar products or services. This will help you determine if you're charging too much or too little.

Also, make sure that your product is unique in some way. The reason why some companies go out of business is that their products look exactly like those of other companies. You need something that sets you apart from everyone else, so that customers have a reason to buy from you instead of your competitors. If it's not unique, then it's not going to be successful because most consumers would rather buy something that looks unique compared to something that looks like every other product on the market.

Now that we've identified who our potential customers are, we can move on to the next step.

Establish a Budget

If you are going to spend money to market your business, you need to be sure your budget[38] is well thought out. You will need to decide how much money you have available for marketing each month and what areas of marketing will receive the majority of that budget.

---

[38] Akhilesh Ganti (updated March 18th 2021)
https://www.investopedia.com/terms/b/budget.asp

Make a list of all the marketing activities that you believe will help promote your business, which ones you can afford and which ones are necessary for success. Once you have decided on a list, prioritize each item on the list so you know what is most important and what can be done later if necessary. Then make a budget for each item on the list based on how much it costs to do and how often it requires doing. Find out who and what can give you the most bang for your buck—one big ad or a series of smaller ads, a billboard or other methods of advertising.

The most important thing about creating a good marketing plan is knowing if all of your targeted customers will see all of your ads, flyers, brochures, etc. If they won't see them or will only see one at best, then you are wasting your money and should rethink how much time and money you spend in this area. While some people think advertising is like buying lottery tickets or gambling, "if I don't try, I don't win," this is not the case for a successful business. A good marketing plan should be an investment in your business, not a gamble on a chance to make it.

For example, if you are a new business, you may not need to buy full-page ads in major newspapers. Your targeted customers may not read those kinds of newspapers. Instead, you may want to start with a less expensive ad or flyers in local newspapers or magazines or local "shopper" papers—a group of small ads that look like a newspaper and are distributed door-to-door. You should also consider advertising on the radio, television and other forms of media that your targeted customers will see and have access to.

Another example, if you are selling a product, is that you may not need to advertise in major magazines. The people that read those magazines are not your targeted customers. You will have a more effective marketing plan if the people who read your ads will be the ones who buy your product.

A good marketing plan is profitable and well planned and will help your business succeed. It is a comprehensive plan that considers all aspects of marketing and what it will take to reach your targeted customers and make money from them. A marketing plan[39] is not a time commitment but a money commitment. If you are going to invest your own money in marketing for the long term, then you might as well invest in producing a quality marketing plan the first time around. Your success depends on it!

Final Tips

Remember that marketing is a process. It does not happen overnight. You must work hard at it for it to be effective. The key to marketing success is that you must reach your targeted audience with your message about your business. Any time you spend planning, researching, and preparing will pay off in the long run. It will save you time and money in the long run.

Make sure your message is clear to everyone who reads or hears it; whether it is a flyer, newspaper ad or brochure. Make sure there are no spelling or grammatical errors, and that

---

[39] Sara McGuire (updated July 16th 2020)
https://venngage.com/blog/marketing-plan

the information is correct and up-to-date. Use pictures whenever possible to help tell your story visually with words alone being secondary.

You want your target customers to know who you are, what you do, how they can reach you and what makes you different from the next guy down the street or across town. You want them to understand why they should buy from you instead of someone else—especially if someone else can offer a cheaper price than yours. This is where all of your hard work comes into play! You have spent countless hours developing an understanding of your customer's needs and wants as well as their buying behavior; now all of this knowledge can be applied to your marketing efforts.

You must be able to tell the whole story quickly and easily. Try different versions of your ads and flyers until you have it down pat. Then test each version on some of your friends or family members who are not related to your business in any way. You want to make sure that they understand what you are trying to say, and that they like the way you are saying it. You can also ask them if they would buy from you based on the information in your ad or flyer.

Remember, most people only read or look at an ad for about ten seconds, so you must make an impact within that period if you want anyone to remember who you are and contact you for more information. So, think about what will get your message across in those ten seconds and then try different ways of saying it until it is perfect for your target audience and gets them to call, visit or buy from you!

Set Marketing Goals

Marketing is a critical part of any business. It's the method used to attract new customers to your business and to keep them coming back. The larger your customer base, the more money you'll make. To get this going, you must set some marketing goals for yourself.

List Your Goals and Why You Want Them

First, figure out what your goals are for marketing your business. What does success look like? Do you want to do a lot of advertising and make more sales? Maybe you just want to get more people in the door or on your mailing list so that they can be notified about upcoming sales or special offers. Whatever it is that you're looking for, create a list of goals and reasons why you want them.

Number Your Goals

Once you've written down your goals, number them in the order you want to achieve them. This will help you to prioritize and focus on the most important items. Keep this list handy, and refer to it daily as you work on your marketing plan.

Make a Template

You should also make a template of all your marketing goals. This will enable you to track how well you're doing on achieving them and help you see what needs more work on your part. You can keep track of your progress by filling in the template every day. It's also a good idea to use a calendar for this so that you can see when you achieve certain goals, such as getting more people on your mailing list.

Review Your Goals

You should also review your marketing goals regularly. At the very least, you should review them once a month and make sure that they're still relevant to your business. If you haven't achieved them yet, then figure out what needs to be done to do so. Don't be afraid to change your goals if external factors change or if your business needs change.

Select Media Channels

This is a key part of setting up your business, as you need to get the message out there to your target audience. You need to have a clear idea of who you're marketing to, as this will help you with identifying the media channels you should use.

When considering who your target audience is, try and think about how far they could travel to get to your business, what sort of income bracket they fall into, where they live (e.g., rural vs. city), whether they're male or female and what age group. This can help you narrow down the exact media channels that will be best for your company.

Here are some examples of media channels you could use:

Print Media – Newspapers, magazines or leaflets. E-zines[40] can also be considered print media if it's in digital format and not online-only e-zine sites such as *Ezine Articles* or *The Hub*.

Television – This could be local news programs, televised commercials on other stations or maybe a talk show.

Radio – How-to programs, news, sports, music, etc.

Internet – This includes everything from websites to online blog posts to social media sites such as Facebook or Twitter. You can even include online classifieds such as Kijiji, internet forums and other formats of internet advertising.

Directories – This could be local Yellow Pages[41] or the White Pages[42].

Advertising – You can advertise in the media channels above or on billboards and other advertising mediums.

Give some thought to what media channels you're going to use for your business. It's a good idea to make a list of them with some notes on how often they're published and where those publications are distributed.

---

[40] Adeel Mehmood (updated December 26th 2019) https://www.benchmarkemail.com/blog/what-are-ezines/
[41] Yellow pages, https://en.wikipedia.org/wiki/Yellow_pages
[42] White pages, https://www.whitepages.com/

This will help you figure out how much it would cost for advertising in each publication, as well as how frequently you should be placing ads (if at all).

For example, if you want to advertise on television but it only runs a few times a week, then it may not be worth your time to place an ad every time it airs. You could instead opt for a larger ad campaign that's spread out over a longer period of time (e.g., monthly).

Develop Strategies and Tactics

This section introduces the reader to the concept of developing strategies and tactics. These terms can be confusing for some because they are used interchangeably. The chapter will emphasize that strategies are long term, whereas tactical planning is short term. Both are critical for the success of any business.

Strategy is a plan for achieving a vision. Like a road map, it provides the direction for how to reach the destination.

Tactical planning is the daily activity of managing and executing strategic plans.

Strategic planning is an ongoing and never-ending process. The success of the plan depends on how far ahead the planner looks and also how well they are able to project what will happen in the future. Tactics are developed to ensure that short-term decisions are made in alignment with the strategic plan.

The section will then introduce you to some of the more popular strategy tools such as SWOT analysis, Porter's five forces[43], and 4P's analysis[44]. There will also be a discussion on how these tools can be used during tactical planning activities to increase your chances of success.

SWOT Analysis

SWOT[45] stands for Strengths, Weaknesses, Opportunities, and Threats. This tool is designed to help determine the opportunities and risks that exist in any given situation. It is also used to identify a company's strengths and weaknesses. This analysis is usually conducted at the corporate level, but it can also be applied on a project level. If you are conducting this analysis for a project level, you must first conduct it at the corporate level, and then translate it to the project level.

Strengths

This section should discuss what has made your company successful in the past. Maybe your company has high quality products or services that no other companies offer. Maybe your company has developed a reputation for being

[43] Porters five forces,
https://www.mindtools.com/pages/article/newTMC_08.htm
[44] Alexandra Twin (updated February 19th 2021)
https://www.investopedia.com/terms/f/four-ps.asp
[45] SWOT analysis, https://en.wikipedia.org/wiki/SWOT_analysis

honest and trustworthy with their clients or customers. Perhaps your company has developed an excellent marketing strategy such as getting free publicity or is able to sell more product than anyone else in your market space because of excellent pricing strategies. There are many reasons why a company may be successful, but they all boil down to one basic concept: the company has found a way to differentiate itself from its competitors.

When conducting a SWOT analysis, it is important to list all of your strengths. There are no disadvantages to identifying your strengths, and most companies will include their weaknesses in this section. A common mistake that companies make is they only identify their weaknesses and fail to mention any of their strengths. Another common mistake is listing generic strengths such as "we have a good reputation" or "we have excellent customer service." While these may be true strengths, they are not specific enough, and often do not provide the reader with any information that will help them determine if your company is successful or not.

For example, if the company is a bakery that bakes only cookies, they may have a strength listed as, "Our chocolate chip cookies are the best." While this is true, it may not help you determine how successful you are as a company. A better strength would be, "Our cookies are hand baked on site using locally sourced ingredients, and our customers love them because we personalize each order with their name."

Weaknesses

The weaknesses section of a SWOT analysis is sometimes the hardest part because most people have an issue with openly discussing their weaknesses. However, it must be done, so that you can identify the areas where you need to improve your business. Common areas where people struggle with identifying weaknesses include management, technology, marketing, operations and other key areas of business. The key here is to identify issues that exist in your business that are preventing you from being successful in some area of your business or preventing you from making money in some area of your business. For example, maybe you find that your employees are spending too much time on the phone with customers. Maybe you find that your office systems are not efficient enough to process all the information you need.

For example, let's say you own a web design company. You may find that your employees are spending too much time generating leads because they are not spending enough time on projects.

The weakness could be related to your business model, the industry in which you compete or something else. The key is to make sure that you have identified one weakness and understand why it is a weakness. If, after doing the analysis, you still feel that your business has no weaknesses, then you can move on to the next section. In my experience working with high-growth startup companies, every business has at least one weakness because businesses have multiple strengths.

Opportunities

The opportunities section of a SWOT analysis is designed to help identify opportunities that exist in the marketplace; opportunities for your company to succeed in areas where others have failed. Not all opportunities are good ones; some may be very risky and should be avoided while others may be low risk but will require a significant investment by the company before it can realize any returns on its investment[46]. An opportunity for one company may only represent a threat for another. The key here is to identify opportunities that will give your company an advantage over competitors in some area of your business or help you make more money in some area of your business.

For example, you may have a product that is unique in some way. Perhaps you have developed a new plastic that is stronger and lighter than anything else on the market. If you are able to market it successfully, this could give you an advantage, since your competition will not be able to create a similar product for some time.

Another example might be if you have an opportunity to enter a new market or expand into an existing market by increasing the capabilities of your company. Perhaps you could purchase another company or develop a new technology that would allow your company to increase its market share or make more money in the markets that it already competes in.

Threats

The threats section of a SWOT analysis is designed to help identify risks that exist in the marketplace; risks that could prevent your company from being successful in areas where

---

[46] Jason Fernando (updated March 1st 2021)
https://www.investopedia.com/terms/r/returnoninvestment.asp

others have been successful. Not all threats are bad; some may be just as good as an opportunity for another company, while others may represent very little threat at all. The key here is to identify threats that will hurt your company in some area of your business or prevent you from making money in some area of your business.

For example, if you are opening a fast-food restaurant, one of the threats may be that your location is too far from a university. This would mean you are not getting the college student business—the biggest group of people who frequent fast-food restaurants.

You need to be sure that you have identified all the threats to your success and eliminated as many as possible before moving forward with your business plan.

4P's Analysis

4P stands for: Product, Price, Place, and Promotion. This tool is used to help determine the market segments that are most profitable for a company. It is also used to identify the products and services that generate the most profit for a company. The 4P tool is most commonly used in strategic planning activities because it helps companies decide which products and services they should offer to their customers based upon their profitability. There are other tools used in strategic planning activities such as SWOT analysis and Porter's five forces, but these three tools will give you all the information needed to conduct a comprehensive strategic planning activity.

Product

The product section of this tool is designed to help identify all of the different products and services offered by a company, how much each product costs to produce, how much each product costs to market, how the customer perceives the product or service, how well the product or service has been received by customers in the past and what percentage of the total sales revenue each product generates. This information is used to identify which products and services are most profitable for a company.

For example, a company could determine that their coffee shop business makes the most profit from selling their roasted coffee beans to local restaurants and bakeries. The company may not have considered selling wholesale coffee beans a viable business opportunity for them. If the 4P analysis revealed that this product generated the most profit, then they would be encouraged to participate in this market with more enthusiasm.

Price

The price section is used to determine what price each product should be sold for, which segments of customers are most profitable and where within this segment of customers a company should place their products and services. This information will be used to develop strategic plans that will help a company increase their sales revenue by focusing on those segments that offer the greatest potential.

For example, if a company is selling a new product, they will want to determine what price they should sell it for. Will it generate more profit if sold to a small segment of customers, or would it be better to sell in large quantities to a larger segment of customers? This information will help the company make the best decision.

Place

The place section is used to determine where products and services are sold, who sells them, and how much it costs to sell them. This information will be used to develop tactical plans that will allow a company to maximize their profitability by identifying those segments where costs can be reduced while maintaining sales volume. There are many ways to reduce costs such as eliminating middlemen or finding less expensive sources for raw materials or labor. There are also opportunities that can be identified for increasing sales volume such as adding new sales outlets or reducing distribution time from suppliers.

Promotion

The promotion section is used to determine how well a company is promoting their products and services. This information will be used to develop tactical plans that will allow a company to increase sales while lowering their marketing costs. There are many ways to promote products and services that do not cost a lot of money. For example, if you have a product that needs to be sold in stores, you can:

Contact the store manager and request a meeting. This will give you an opportunity to explain your product or service and how it could benefit them as well as their customers. If they are not interested, ask if they know of anyone within their chain of command in another store who might be more inclined to listen. The key here is persistence! When approaching the store manager, always use the telephone first because it is less confrontational and easier to end the conversation without upsetting the other person. If you approach the store manager face-to-face for the first time, then you may never get an opportunity for a second meeting unless they contact you first. Many times, this will happen, but on average it is better if you make the effort to call before showing up at their office or store location. You do not want your first and only meeting to be on their turf.

Give away free samples[47] of your product or service. This is a great way to get your foot in the door. If you can get customers to try your product, then they may be more inclined to buy it. The main thing is not to give away too many free samples because this will make the store manager question how much profit you are making by selling your product or service. If you are selling a product that is low-cost, they will expect you to sell it for less than what it costs you to produce and market the item. If you are selling a high-cost item, they will expect you to sell it for more than what it costs you to produce and market the item. The key here is that if you have a high profit margin on any one item, that particular item should be sold in fewer locations with less of an emphasis on

---

[47] Product sample, https://en.wikipedia.org/wiki/Product_sample

giving out free samples because this will cause immediate suspicion of your motives by the store manager.

Contact the store manager and ask them how sales are for their current inventory of products or services. You may find out that they has already tried selling your existing products, but they could use some new ideas on how they can use them best within his location. This is a win-win situation because you could gain an account for your existing product or you could develop an entirely new product by combining your existing product with something that the store manager is currently selling.

Ask them if they would be interested in selling your products or services. You may find out that they have been waiting for someone like you to come along and offer them a better price on their current inventory of products or services.

Ask them if they would be interested in working with you to develop a new product that combines both of your products into one. This scenario can be very profitable because it allows you to offer two products in one location at a lower cost than if they were sold separately. The key is that both products must be somewhat related, or they will not sell together. For example, if one product is low cost then try offering higher cost related items at the same location or within close proximity to each other. If one product is high profit, then try offering low profit related items at the same location or within close proximity to each other and see how well they sell together before adding additional unrelated items to this mix. Keep in mind that stores are always looking for ways to increase sales and profit, so they might be willing to work with you to develop a new product if you can offer them a better profit margin than what they are currently making on their own products.

Chapter 5: Sales and Distribution

Sales and Distribution encompass all the activities involved in getting a product to market. Several business functions are involved in sales and distribution, including:

- Marketing—introducing the product to the customer
- Sales—the activity of convincing the customer to purchase the product
- Delivery—delivering the finished good to the customer's location or installation at a location specified by the customer.

Sales and Distribution may also be known as "Marketing & Sales."

Marketing and Sales are functions of the Sales and distribution Department. The Sales and Distribution Department are concerned with getting products to market, hence the term "Marketing." The Marketing function is customer-oriented, which means that it focuses on customer needs. Sales and Distribution personnel are concerned with making sure that all the steps required to get a product to market have been taken. They are also responsible for making sure that the product is shipped properly, at the right time and for the right price. Sales and Distribution personnel are responsible for maintaining good relationships with customers so that orders will continue to be placed in the future. They also ensure that customers receive order information in a timely manner.

When a company has more than one product, each product is generally handled by a separate section of Sales and Distribution personnel (e.g., there may be separate sections for personal computers, printers, or other computer accessories). In addition, there may be several different departments involved in getting a single product to market (e.g., there might be separate departments for Marketing and Advertising (Marketing), Pricing, Research and Development[48] (R&D), Production Planning and Control[49] (PPC), Production (Manufacturing), and Sales.

Sales and Distribution personnel must be able to deal with all the different departments within the organization so that orders are processed properly. They must also be able to handle customers. The person who is responsible for managing the Sales and Distribution Department is called a "Distribution Manager."

We will go into these concepts more completely in this chapter.

---

[48] Will Kenton (updated July 5tht 2020)
https://www.investopedia.com/terms/r/randd.asp
[49] Venkatesh,
https://www.yourarticlelibrary.com/management/planning-management/production-planning-and-control-meaning-characteristics-and-objectives/53145

People Who Buy

Firstly, the person who buys the product is the consumer. The consumer is the one who buys the product and makes use of it.

The next person we come across is the provider. The provider is the producer or seller of a product. They supply it to the consumers. They take care that their product satisfies the consumers so that they can and will buy it again and again. They have to make sure that they have a good relationship with their customers, so that they will come back to them whenever they need a product of their kind.

Lastly, there is one more person involved in this transaction: a middleman[50] or broker, whose job is to mediate between the seller and buyer in order to facilitate transactions between them. This person, though not necessary for all products, can be very helpful when there are many different products involved or if there are many different parties buying and selling at once (like stock exchanges). They may also be charged with maintaining records about everything related to sales in order to aid future transactions involving this product (this can include things like how many units were sold, to who, how much was paid for each unit, etc.).

Difference Between Marketing and Sales

The sales and distribution process can be divided into two main parts: the marketing process and the actual sale.

---

[50] Adam Hayes (updated January 7th 2021)
https://www.investopedia.com/terms/m/middleman.asp

The marketing process is where the producer promotes his product to potential customers. This can be done in numerous ways like through advertising, word of mouth, publicity and other forms of media.

After this promotion, there is a period of time called the "selling season[51]," when the producer actually makes his sales.

The actual sale is when the consumer decides to purchase products from a particular provider or seller. The provider wants to make sure that they have good relationships with their customers (so that they will come back and buy from them again), so they tries to keep them satisfied with their product or service.

If the customer is satisfied, he or she is likely to buy products from this provider again in the future. However, if he/she does not like what he/she gets or finds it too expensive, or if there are no other reasons for him/her to return, then there is no point in buying from this provider again. It will be useless for both him/her and the provider because they have already established a relationship, and they have nothing more to gain from each other.

For example, a customer comes to the store, tries out one of the products and decides to buy it. The provider (the shopkeeper) will give a price for the product that may or may not be agreeable to the buyer. If it is agreeable, he/she takes it

---

[51] Selling season
https://www.weconnectfashion.com/articles/selling-seasons

and pays for it. If not, he/she can go somewhere else to look for a better deal.

In order to ensure that customers are satisfied with their purchase, there are some things that providers can do:

Firstly, they can keep good relationships with their customers so that they will come back when they need more products of this kind.

This can be done by giving good customer service and by keeping their prices low. They also try to keep their products fresh (by putting in preservatives/refrigeration, etc.) so that they will not go bad (and spoil) before the consumer uses them or sells them off.

Providers also make sure their products are in good condition when they sell them because good quality products will make sure that the consumer is satisfied with what he/she gets (even if he/she gets a lower priced product).

If something goes wrong with his/her purchase, the consumer can go back and tell his/her provider about it and work out an agreement between them both on how best to resolve the problem. A provider will do anything to make sure that their customers are kept happy, and this will ensure that they come back to them again and again.

Secondly, producers also give their products a good package so that customers will be able to recognize them easily when they are buying.

They also mark their product in such a way that it is distinguished from other products (usually by putting their own brand name on it). This is so consumers can easily recognize what they want when they come to the shops to buy.

Producers also label their products with information such as how much it weighs, what ingredients are used and other key factors. This is so the consumer can read up about the product before buying it.

This is also important because different consumers buy different things for different reasons. Some people buy food because of its taste, while others buy food because of its health value (like vitamins or minerals).

So, producers have to make sure that these kinds of consumers know about the details of their product so there will be no misunderstandings or confusion on behalf of the consumer. For example, if someone buys food because he/she wants something nutritious but finds out later that their "healthy" food has just as much cholesterol as junk food, he/she will probably not buy that product again.

The producer also marks their products with information such as how to store them and how long they will last after they are purchased by the consumer. They do this because if the consumer knows how long their product will last, then he/she will be able to use it or sell it off before it goes bad, which will make him/her happy. If the consumer uses up the product before it goes bad, then he/she cannot be criticized for being wasteful.

This is also why there are some products like toothpaste and medicines that need to be sold within a limited number of years (because they have an expiration date) because if you don't use them up before that date, they go bad.

Thirdly, producers have to keep in mind that their product has to be consistent and reliable in order for customers to keep coming back for more of the same.

This means they have to make sure that their product is not subject to too much variation because if there is too much variation the customer may end up buying a different brand next time. He/she will think his previous purchase was no good and want a better experience next time around.

This also means that producers need to maintain good quality control standards[52] so that they will not sell their product to the customer if it is of bad quality.

Lastly, producers have to make sure that their products are affordable for the consumer because if they are not, then they will have a hard time selling them. This means they have to take into account all of the costs involved in producing the product and add on a bit extra, so that they can earn money from it.

Producers also have to consider the prices set by other producers of similar products and use these as a standard when setting their own prices. This is so that consumers will be able to compare prices of different products offered by different

[52] Quality standards https://asq.org/quality-resources/learn-about-standards

sellers and choose what works out as the best deal for them in order to buy it.

How Much to Sell

Now that the first step in the sales cycle has been completed, it is time to sell. In order to do this, a company must determine how much of its product or service to sell.

There are basically three ways to decide how much to sell:

Limit sales (in quantity)

This is a fairly common practice for businesses that have legal or regulatory requirements or limitations on the number of sales they can make. For example, a company that sells alcoholic beverages may be required by law to have a certain percentage of its total sales be made up of non-alcoholic beverages (this prevents alcoholics from becoming dependent on alcohol). Businesses also set limits on their total sales as part of their marketing strategy. For example, many software companies limit the number of licenses they will sell for their products.

Limit sales (in dollars)

This method is often used when a business wants to control its profits and expenses. For example, a business may limit its income by only selling products at $10 per item in order to ensure it does not make more profit than it needs to survive or pay off debts incurred during startup. The limiting factor in this case is the price at which the product is sold rather than the number of units sold.

Determine the price based on a value proposition

This is the preferred method of many businesses. In this case, the business determines what value the product or service will provide to the consumer and sets its price based on that value. For example, if a business is selling a new software program to help consumers create web sites, it may sell its product at $100 per license because it believes that $100 is a reasonable value for creating a website (in addition to any other benefits the program provides).

After deciding how much to sell in total, you must now decide how much of that product or service your sales force will sell.

This is known as the sales mix[53], and there are no set rules for determining what this should be. Most companies will decide on a percentage of total sales for each category (for example, 80% on-site and 20% off-site).

However, it is important to be aware that you can have different sales mixes for each product or service that your company sells, and some products may have more than one way of being sold (for example, some software products can be purchased online but also have an on-site version).

---

[53] Will Kenton (updated May 7th 2019)
https://www.investopedia.com/terms/s/sales-mix.asp

In these cases, you must decide how much of each version to offer to the market. The sales mix is generally determined by a company's marketing strategy and may be set based on how much a company believes it can sell of each product or service.

Pricing Strategy

Once you have decided how much of each product or service to sell, you must now price it. Pricing is an important strategic decision that will affect your sales and profitability.

There are five pricing strategies that are used in deciding the price of a product or service:

Cost-plus

This pricing method involves adding an additional amount (the markup[54]) to the cost of producing/selling the product. The markup is added in order to account for any additional costs over what it costs the company to produce/sell the product (for example, overhead[55] costs). This method is not used very often because it does not take into account other factors that affect price such as demand, competition, etc. However, this method is sometimes used for internal products where there is no competition and no consideration need be given to what competitors charge for similar products.

---

[54] Markup, https://en.wikipedia.org/wiki/Markup_(business)
[55] Alicia Tuovila (updated March 23rd 2021) https://www.investopedia.com/terms/o/overhead.asp

Competition-based

This pricing strategy involves setting prices based on what competitors charge for similar products/services. For example, if Company X offers one type of software program at $150 per license and another company offers its program at $100 per license, Company X may determine that it should set its price at $120 per license to maintain profits. There are many disadvantages with this strategy, including that competitors may be charging more than they need to for their products (this may be due to high overhead costs or a competitive strategy); competitors may be able to sell more of a product at a lower price (which can lead to greater sales); and competitors may be hurting your business by charging too little for their products/services.

Value-based

This pricing strategy involves setting prices based on the value provided by the product or service. This strategy is the preferred method of most businesses because it is the most customer-focused strategy available. Essentially, a company will decide what value it can give customers and then charge them an amount that is reasonable for what they are getting in return. For example, if a business decides that its software product will help users create web sites more efficiently than competitors' products, it will set its price at $100 per license, because users find this price reasonable given that they can create sites much faster than before. This method has many advantages over the competition-based pricing strategy, including that it looks like the company is providing a valuable service for a reasonable price, and it does not involve competitors in the decision-making process.

Cost-based

This pricing strategy involves setting prices based on the cost of producing/selling the product with no extra markup. This is generally considered a "no-win" situation for a company, as it will not make any profit due to the high cost involved in producing/selling the product. However, this strategy can be useful if you are trying to sell a product or service that has very low overhead costs (for example, if you are selling software that only requires internet access and is relatively cheap to produce). However, be aware that customers will likely find your price unreasonable given the lack of value provided by your product/service and may decide not to purchase from you at all.

Promotion-based

This pricing strategy involves basing your price on how much it will cost you to promote the product (for example, through advertising or promotion). The advantage of this method is that it allows businesses to set prices based on how much they want to spend promoting their products rather than basing their prices on what their competitors charge for similar products/services. There are many disadvantages with this strategy, including that competition may offer promotions at a lower cost than you can, your prices may be higher than your competitors' prices even if you offer a comparable product/service and you are not taking into account how much value your product/service actually provides to customers (which may lead to low sales).

Once you have determined how much of each product or service to sell, and how much of that product or service will be sold on-site or off-site, it is time to determine what price to sell it for. This is known as setting the price. The pricing strategy that you use will affect the final price. You should not assume that your pricing strategy will remain the same from year-to-year (as your business may change), so it is important to review your pricing strategy at least once a year if not more often.

Where to Sell

For your business to succeed, you must find a place to sell your product or service. This is where the marketplace comes in. A marketplace is simply where people buy and sell goods and services.

You must think carefully about what kind of marketplace will best suit your business. There are four different types of marketplaces, each with its own advantages and disadvantages.

Direct Sales

You make a direct sale to the person buying the product or service. Direct sales involve a personal relationship between buyer and seller. The advantage of direct sales is that you can see the face of the person you are selling to, ask questions about why he or she wants your product or service, and take time to explain why it will be helpful for that person. The disadvantage of direct sales is that you may have difficulty finding enough people who want what you're selling at any given time.

For example, you might sell ice cream in your neighborhood. You would have to convince the people in your community that they want to buy frozen treats from you, and you would have to deliver your ice cream to their homes or offices.

If you want to sell your product or service by direct sale, consider these rules:

- Make sure the people who buy from you are ready and willing to pay for what you sell.
- Make sure you can deliver what you promise.
- Make sure you have a good reputation. You must convince people that they can trust you to be honest, to keep your word, and to do what you say you'll do.

Indirect Sales

You sell through a third-party agent[56] who then sells your product or service on behalf of you and your business. The advantage of this type of sale is that it expands the number of people who can buy directly from you as well as opens up new markets for entry into foreign countries, huge companies and other platforms, that might not otherwise allow direct

---

[56] Third party agent, https://www.lawinsider.com/dictionary/third-party-agent

sales. The disadvantage of indirect sales is that you have little or no control over how your product or service is sold, sometimes for a lower price than you prefer.

For example, you might sell your product to a department store, who then sells the product to their customers. When you sell products or services through an agent or third-party (an individual or company that isn't part of your business), you have almost no control over how the product is sold.

Subsidiary Sales

You sell goods through another company to a third party. For example, you could sell your product through a wholesaler or distributor to other stores that then sell the product to the final customer. The advantage of this type of sale is that it allows you to penetrate markets that would otherwise not allow direct sales. It lets you enter huge companies that might not allow direct selling or creates openings into foreign countries and huge companies that might not otherwise allow direct selling. The disadvantage is that your business may have little control over how the goods are sold.

For example, you might have an assembly line at your plant, and you hire someone to put together your product. You pay the person $8 per hour to assemble the product. You might then sell that product to a wholesaler for $12 per unit, and the wholesaler sells the product to a retailer for $16 per unit. The disadvantage of this type of sale is that you will lose money on each sale because you are not making as much as you could if you sold the product yourself.

Retail Sales

You sell directly to the final customer at retail stores[57] where your customers go to have things done for them while they wait. For example, there are many hair salons where the customers sit in chairs and wait for their haircuts while they read magazines about celebrities' lives or watch television shows on which people try out new products in front of cameras; then they pay for their cuts when they're done with them. The advantage of retail sales is immediacy; your customer can get what he or she wants right away. The disadvantage is that you must deal with the customers directly, since there is no intermediary to go through.

For example, if you decide to open a business that sells and delivers flowers, you will want to choose a retail sales strategy. You will have to deal directly with the customers who buy your flowers, creating a personal relationship between you and them.

Many Businesses Grow by Expanding Their Sales and Distribution Networks

A business might start out by getting its products into ten stores in its local community. After it has done that

---

[57] Retail store, https://accountlearning.com/retail-store-meaning-types-of-retail-stores/

successfully, it could expand its distribution network by selling to different stores in other cities or even countries.

For example, a business started by a man named John Mackey[58] in Austin, Texas, eventually became Whole Foods Market. In the beginning, he worked as a cashier at an organic food store. After learning what it took to run the business, he opened his own store with one employee and $10,000[59] as borrowed money. Then he expanded the business by opening two new stores.

Now, Whole Foods Market[60] is a large chain of stores selling organic food all over the United States and even in some foreign countries.

Channel Responsibility

Sales and Distribution is the channel of your business that gives you the opportunity to bring your product or service to the market. When you sell, you need a company that can distribute your product to customers in a convenient and efficient manner.

The sales and distribution channel includes all suppliers, manufacturers, distributors and retailers who bring goods to the customer. It's important to remember that when selecting your sales channel, you need not only their marketing and distribution capabilities, but also their financial stability. If they can't meet their bills, how can they pay yours?

---

[58] John Mackey,
https://en.wikipedia.org/wiki/John_Mackey_(businessman)
[59] Career of John Mackey,
https://en.wikipedia.org/wiki/John_Mackey_(businessman)
[60] Whole Foods Market, https://wholefoodsmarket.comt.com

In addition, don't overlook the importance of finding a sales channel partner with whom you're comfortable doing business. You need someone who is reliable who will give your products proper representation.

The sales and distribution channel is an important part of your business. You need to develop a solid relationship with the partners in your sales channel. You need to know them, and they need to know you. They should know your product or service as well as they know their own.

When you work with sales and distribution channels, be prepared to make a substantial investment of time and money. It will take time to build trusting relationships. It will take time for your partner to learn about you, your product or service, and how it is different from the rest of the marketplace. It will take time for them to establish their position in the marketplace as an expert in your field.

Make sure that this channel is committed to creating relationships that last over time and not just making a short-term sale[61].

Marketing

Marketing involves establishing the value proposition of what you have for sale, getting others interested in what you have for sale, getting people who are interested in what you

---

[61] Julia Kagan (updated January 29th 2021)
https://www.investopedia.com/terms/s/short-term-gain.asp

have for sale to buy it from your company and delivering it so that they are satisfied with their purchase—all at a profit for your company!

Marketing is more than just advertising. Advertising is just one of the many things you must do to achieve good marketing.

Get the word out about what you have for sale by using marketing communications such as brochures, flyers, advertising in newspapers, magazines, on television and on the Internet. Price your product or service properly and make it available through distribution channels like mail order catalogs and Internet websites.

The goal of marketing is to attract customers who buy because they want your products or services, so pick your company's target market carefully. If you don't know who your market is, you can't sell to them!

Marketing communications[62] can be expensive, but they are the most effective way to create interest in your product or service. Once you have developed a marketing plan, be sure to monitor it to make sure that you are getting the results you want.

The responsibility for marketing is yours. No one else can do it for you.

---

[62] Marketing communication,
https://en.wikipedia.org/wiki/Marketing_communications

Distribution

Distribution is the process of getting products or services from the manufacturer or producer to the consumer. In other words, it is making sure that your product gets to the place where it can be sold. The cost of distribution is one of the main factors that distinguish a low-cost business from a high-cost business—and high cost means you make less profit!

When you are developing products, pick a product that will minimize your costs of distribution. For instance, if you are selling food by mail order, then choose foods that don't spoil easily and don't need refrigeration. If you have a service that can be performed over the Internet, then consider how much time and money it would take to get the service from where you live to where your client lives before deciding on what kind of service to offer!

Distribution Channel

The distribution channel[63] consists of all those organizations who receive your product or service and then distribute it to its final destination: customers who will buy your product or service.

The key point in selecting a distribution channel is finding someone who will sell your product at a reasonable price and in a reasonable amount of time.

---

[63] Jason Fernando (updated January 24th 2021)
https://www.investopedia.com/terms/d/distribution-channel.asp

The problem with this channel is that there are so many players in the distribution channel that it can be difficult to know who to work with. You need to know what products or services each of them offers, and how good they are at getting your product to the market. You also need to know their reputation for honesty and reliability.

Consider whether you want your product and service delivered in person or by mail order catalogs, over the Internet or through other means such as home shopping networks. Consider how much time it will take for your customers to get the product and whether they will be happy with your product once they get it. Consider whether you can trust this channel partner to pay you when they should do so. Make sure that this channel partner is willing to work with you as a partner in your business—not just a supplier of your product or service!

It's also important that you keep in touch with every part of your distribution channel—from manufacturing through purchase by the customer—so that things go smoothly at all times. If something goes wrong, then fix it before it gets worse!

Retailers

Retailers provide direct contact between manufacturers and consumers through their stores, catalogs, mail order operations, telemarketing and the Internet.

Retailers sell your products through their own sales force, or they can work with other distributors such as wholesalers or jobbers to get your product into their stores.

When you are selecting a retailer, you need to find a retailer who is willing to work with you in promoting your product. If you are selling a new product, then you need someone who is willing to help you develop the market for it. You need someone who will take the time to understand how your product works and why people want it.

It's also important that this channel partner has access to customers who will buy your product and is willing to represent it in a positive way.

The best way for retailers to make money is by keeping operating costs low and selling as much inventory as possible—so be sure that they are committed to using good marketing methods such as direct mail, telemarketing, advertising and other methods of promoting the sale of your products! It's not enough just to have a good product—retailers must know how to sell it!

Manufacturers

A manufacturer is the company that makes your product. This might be you, but it could also be someone else—and you might even already have a manufacturer selected as part of your business plan.

When you are looking for a manufacturer, you need to find one who will produce your product or service in the quantities you need at the price you want. You need a manufacturer who has access to your market and who has contacts with customers who are willing to buy and use your product. You need someone who will work with you on promoting and selling your product so that it is attractive to customers and easy for them to obtain. You also need someone with whom working is pleasant!

It's not enough just to get an acceptable price from the manufacturer—they must also treat their customers well! The manufacturers of many high-quality products are known for their superior customer service!

Suppliers

A supplier provides goods or services that help fill out or enhance the value of what your business offers. They could be providers of raw materials, parts or equipment, or they could provide additional services that help make things go more smoothly in other areas of your business. Suppliers can also include partners such as banks, consultants, and accountants.

When you are selecting suppliers, you need to find ones who will provide what you need at a price that is fair and who will deliver on time. You also need to find ones who will work with you in developing your business so that their services help make it stronger!

You may want to look for suppliers who have a good reputation for providing quality products and services. This may mean paying a little more, but it could also mean lower costs down the road if something goes wrong, and it could lead to happier customers!

Controlling Distribution Channels

The marketing strategy devised by the organization will be carried out through various channels, and it is imperative that the organization exercises control over these channels.

The organization can control its distribution channels in the following ways:

Ownership and Operational Control of Distribution Channels

Ownership of Distribution Channels

The firm may own its distribution channels (e.g., a firm may own its own retail outlets, or a hospital may run its own ambulances) which are called owned distribution channels. As such, the firm has direct control over these physical facilities, giving the firm effective control over the channel.

For example, if a retail outlet is damaged due to some calamity or theft, then it can be repaired or replaced easily by the firm itself without depending on other firms for doing so.

Operational Control of Distribution Channels

In some cases, the firm does not necessarily have ownership of its distribution channels but has operational control over them, which means that it controls their operations directly and indirectly through contract or other methods like maintaining exclusive contracts with them or sponsoring them in exchange for certain services rendered by them in promoting goods produced by the firm.

For example, primary goals of the Coca-Cola[64] company are not the sale and distribution of its product, but rather to maintain and promote the business as a whole through sponsorship of sporting events[65], entertainment shows, concerts and other media sources.

Financial Control of Distribution Channels

This is achieved by carrying out the following:

Subsidies and Grants

The firm may take the responsibility of distributing its products by providing subsidies and grants to the channels, which are given in exchange for certain activities done by them in marketing the firm's goods. For example, a firm gives subsidies to its dealers for promoting its products during off-peak hours. This can be done through different methods such as cash payments, loans at reduced interest rates or free or cheap supplies of goods (e.g., during off-peak hours when sales are low). The firm may also provide inducements such as prizes or awards to motivate its distributors to promote its products.

---

[64] Coco-Cola, https://www.coca-colacompany.com/
[65] Sponsorships, https://www.coca-colacompany.com/company/history/coca-cola-sponsorships

For example, a firm may give prizes to its distributors who manage to sell more units of a product than other dealers do. In another case, a sports equipment manufacturer provides prizes to distributors who sell more units of sports equipment in their district than others do. This encourages the distributor to use his/her best efforts in marketing the product effectively and earn valuable prizes in return.

Credit facilities

These can be given either directly by the firm itself (e.g., a bank may give credit facilities to its dealers so that they can purchase more units of the firm's products) or through financial institutions that are controlled by the firm (e.g., a firm may establish a finance facility for its distributors, in which case it will only advance credit to them on the basis of their future sales performance). These facilities may be given at a reduced interest rate to motivate distributors to purchase more units of goods produced by the firm.

For example, we can take the example of a branded FMCG[66] product. The brand owner will sell the product to the distributor at a price equivalent to their cost plus some margin and also give them credit facility. This credit facility will be given on the basis of future sales performance.

Control over investment

---

[66] Will Kenton (updated March 8th 2021)
https://www.investopedia.com/terms/f/fastmoving-consumer-goods-fmcg.asp

The firm controls investment activities of channels through various means such as: (i) deciding the amount of funds that should be invested in distribution activities, (ii) deciding where and when funds should be directed, (iii) specifying what types of investments in distribution activities should be made and (iv) specifying the terms and conditions on which funds should be lent to distributors or dealers.

For example, a car manufacturer specifies that only those dealers who have sponsored motor races in their district can purchase new cars from it at reduced rates. This serves as an incentive for dealers to sponsor motor races.

Control over distribution costs

The organization exercises control over costs incurred by its distributors and channels by providing them with various incentives such as cash payments or free services, etc., in exchange for them lowering their anticipated costs for the firm's products. For example, a firm may provide free or cheap spare parts to dealers for a period of time in exchange for them reducing their anticipated costs to the firm.

In another example, a computer maker distributes its products through channel partners which include dealers. The manufacturer offers free support to dealers for a period of time in exchange for them not lowering the anticipated cost of the firm's products.

Control over promotion

The organization controls its promotion expenses by specifying how and when such funds should be used by distributors or dealers; generally, it also specifies the terms and conditions on which funds should be given to them like determining in advance how much money should be spent on various forms of promotion (e.g., advertisement) at different stages of distribution system (e.g., at the manufacturer's level, at the wholesale level, and at the retail level).

For example, a manufacturer may give the dealers only fifty percent of the money they need to execute a specific promotional campaign. The remaining amount is given only on the condition that they must spend the amount in promoting the product exactly as required by the company.

Control Over Information

The organization can exercise control over information related to their products in several ways such as:

Quality control

To ensure that information about its goods provided by distributor/s is reliable, a firm may inspect their packaging facilities, etc., and may even specify quality control standards that must be maintained in these facilities so that they are able to maintain high standards of quality in packaging produced by them; if they fail to comply with these standards, they might have their contracts with the company revoked or any incentives given to them taken back.

For example, if a company is selling watches, it may specify that the firm must comply with the standards of watchmaking specified by the Swiss Standards Institute.

Control of product differentiation

A firm may also control the quality of information provided by distributors about its products by specifying its standards for product differentiation[67] and setting up inspection systems[68] to ensure that its distributors adhere to these standards.

For example, a firm may specify that it would like to sell its products in different sizes such as adult, junior, and child size. It can announce that the firm will conduct regular inspections during the year to ensure that each dealer is not marketing all three sizes in his/her store at the same time; this would enable the firm to maintain high standards of product differentiation.

Control over price information

The organization can control price information provided by distributors and dealers by specifying in advance how much money should be spent on advertising prices or how many units should be sold at each price level, for different periods

---

[67] Carol M.Kopp (updated March 3rd 2021)
https://www.investopedia.com/terms/p/product_differentiation.asp
[68] Inspection systems, https://www.stemmer-imaging.com/en/knowledge-base/vision-system/

of time (e.g., for a month or a week). This would help it maintain high standards of price information dissemination.

For example, the company may order its distributors to sell at a certain price, or it may instruct dealers to maintain a price at a certain level.

Control over promotional activities

The organization can control promotional activities related to its products which are undertaken by distributors or dealers by specifying what types of promotional activities should be undertaken (e.g., it may specify that only one type of promotional activity should be undertaken at a time) and how and when these activities should be carried out (e.g., it may specify that a certain amount of money should be spent on one or more types of promotional activities).

For example, an organization can specify: a certain type of packaging that should be used by the distributors, a certain color for the packaging material that should be used by the distributors, a certain type of advertisement that should be used for promoting its product, a certain period of time when the advertising campaign should be carried out and a certain amount of money that each distributor or dealer must spend on advertising over a specified period of time.

Control Over the Organization's Image

The organization can control the image of its products among its distributors and dealers in several ways such as:

Identifying image problems

The firm may identify problems such as poor-quality products, misleading information[69] about products and other vital information, which cause its products to have a negative image among distributors or dealers. It can then take steps to improve these problems.

For example, a firm may find that false information about its products has been given to consumers by one of its distributors; it then issues a statement explaining to consumers that this is not true so that the distributor's reputation is not damaged in the eyes of consumers.

Control over product quality

If there are some deficiencies in product quality which have been identified at the manufacturing stage, then the firm can specify quality control standards for each stage of the distribution system so that these deficiencies are corrected before they reach the hands of consumers.

For example, if there are some defective units produced by the firm which are delivered to its distributors, it can then specify that these defective units should be replaced by the firm itself or by its dealers.

Control over information

---

[69] False information, https://www.lawinsider.com/dictionary/false-information

The organization may take steps to ensure that the information given on its products is not less than what is promised. For example, if a firm promises to give a one-year guarantee on its products, then it must be made sure that consumers are provided with this guarantee.

For example, Nestle[70] and Colgate[71] advertise that their products are manufactured in hygienic conditions and guarantee that the product will be free from any adulteration. The companies may take steps to check whether this promise is being fulfilled or not. For example, samples of the product may be taken randomly for testing, and if any adulteration is found, it should be reported to the consumers.

Control over promotion

The organization may also specify in advance how much should be spent on promoting its products at various stages of the distribution system, so that promotional activities are carried out according to plan, and high standards of image are maintained in the eyes of consumers for different periods of time (e.g., for a month or for a week).

Control Over the Organization's Relationship with Channels

The organization can control the relationship between it and its channels in several ways such as:

Selecting and recruiting distributors

To ensure that distributors who are selected by it have a high probability of successfully marketing the firm's products, the firm can hire external organizations like an advertising agency[72] or an external consultant[73] to carry out research in order to find out about their success rates; this research would include the following:

- The track records of these distributors, including the success rates of their past products.
- The history of the distributors, e.g., the kind of services they have provided to other organizations in the past.

Training distributors

The organization may also train its distributors to make them aware of strategies and tactics used by other organizations to keep them competitive.

Monitoring distributor performance

---

[72] Advertising agency,
https://en.wikipedia.org/wiki/Advertising_agency
[73] External consultant,
https://www.betterevaluation.org/en/evaluation-options/ExternalConsultant

The organization can specify the performance standards it wants from its distributors in the following ways:

- Require all distributors to send regular reports on their sales and feedback on product quality, service levels, etc., to the organization so that any problems can be identified and rectified at an early stage.
- Carry out regular inspections of the distribution channel to check whether it is following the standards set for it or not; visiting its dealers at periodic intervals is one way of doing this.

Removing poor performing dealers

If some of the firm's dealers are not performing well, then they should be removed from the distribution channel by either taking back their franchises or terminating contracts with them; both of these methods should be used in this order according to the seriousness of these problems (e.g., if a dealer is failing to sell a firm's products for a long time, then he should first be asked for an explanation which he should give within a specified time period; if he fails to do so, then his franchise or contract should be terminated).

For example, Kodak[74] has been able to control its distribution channels by removing poor performing dealers. According to (Collins, 1995), Kodak[75] has had great success in its control of its distribution channels by being able to control both the distributors and dealers. By doing this, it was able to

---

[74] Kodak, https://www.kodak.com/en/
[75] Jordan Crook, https://techcrunch.com/2012/01/21/what-happened-to-kodaks-moment/

maintain high dealer concentration which enabled it to have more effective control over them than its competitors (e.g., Fuji[76]).

Terminating bad relationships

If the organization has a bad relationship with all its dealers, then it may terminate all its contracts with them and appoint new dealers who are likely to perform better.

Increasing the number of distributors

The organization can also increase the number of distributors for its products, so that they will have higher visibility in the market; this can be done by either:

- Introducing new products in the market which are similar to the existing ones so that these products appeal to different groups of people and can be marketed by different distributors.
- Promoting a product through several channels at the same time so that it gets enough exposure in the market. For example, if a firm is selling its products through a direct marketing channel as well as through an indirect channel, then it may use both these channels simultaneously to promote its products in order to increase its sales volume; this will also increase

---

[76] The Kodak-Fuji rivalry,
https://www.icmrindia.org/casestudies/catalogue/Business%20strategy1/Business%20Strategy%20The%20Kodak%20-%20Fuji%20Rivalry.htm

the number of consumers who know about its products and can thus purchase them when required.

Terminating good relationships

The organization may also terminate the contracts with its distributors if they are performing well and there is no need to remove them from the distribution channel. For example, if a firm has some very loyal dealers who are selling its products very well and can be expected to continue doing so, then it may not want to terminate them even if it faces some problems with other dealers in its distribution channel.

Control Over the Organization's Channels of Communication

The organization can control the channels of communication in which it communicates with its distributors and consumers in several ways such as:

Selecting channels of communication

The organization should select channels of communication that are most appropriate for the product category or for the type of product that is being distributed by it (e.g., through a direct marketing channel or through an indirect channel).

For example, if a product is sold through a retail outlet or supermarket, then electronic media such as radio, TV, or newspaper advertisements will not be appropriate; these media will be appropriate for products which are sold through a mail-order catalogue. Similarly, for products which are sold on the

Internet, print media will not be appropriate; these media will be appropriate for products which are sold through a telephone call center line.

Selecting media

The organization should select the appropriate media for each channel of communication that it uses, particularly when communicating with consumers.

For example, if a firm is selling its products through a direct marketing channel where it wants to communicate with its distributors, then it should use electronic media such as radio or TV; in this case, the organization should not use print media such as newspapers or magazines because these are not suitable for communicating information efficiently to large numbers of people at the same time. On the other hand, if it wants to communicate with consumers, then print media such as brochures are more appropriate than electronic media like radio or TV because the print media can be used to communicate detailed information about products and services in an attractive manner which cannot be done through electronic media.

For example, McDonald's[77] is a multinational fast-food restaurant chain which maintains a large database of potential customers and uses direct marketing[78] to communicate with them. The company selects appropriate

---

[77] McDonalds, https://www.mcdelivery.co.in/
[78] Marketing strategies, https://postfunnel.com/mcdonalds-marketing-strategy-staying-transparent-while-under-fire/

media such as TV, radio, and magazines to communicate with its customers to develop their brand image.

Communicating regularly

The organization should also specify in advance how often it will communicate with its distributors and consumers so that they do not feel ignored by the firm; this can be done by specifying:

- The frequency of communication and what will be conveyed in each communication (e.g., once a week, once a month); what the content of each communication will be (e.g., sales information, new product information, coupons or vouchers for promotional offers).
- The time of each communication (e.g., the time when faxes to distributors will be sent out, the time when a mailer will be delivered to consumers).

For example, if a firm sends out a mailer to its consumers once every two weeks, then it should also send out a follow-up communication with new information to the same consumers within four to seven days of the earlier communication so that they do not feel ignored or forgotten by the firm.

Chapter 6: Business Strategy

Strategy is the plan for a business to achieve its overall corporate objectives and mission statement. The strategy will indicate what products and services the company will offer, who will be the customers, and what kind of marketing activities the company will use.

In most cases, businesses are started with a well-thought-out strategy. The strategy and the business plan to support it will be the guide for the company's actions and directions in the future.

In this chapter, I will share with you the elements of a good strategy and demonstrate how to apply the strategy for your business.

What Is Strategy?

The definition of "strategy" in Merriam-Webster's Collegiate Dictionary is: "the art of devising and employing plans of action to achieve a long-range goal." A strategy is the plan to achieve a goal.

A good business strategy will enable you to reach your goals in a shorter period of time and with less effort. It will also provide you with concrete actions that you can take to achieve your goals. It is a valuable tool in the hands of the business owner.

Strategy is a critical element in the success of any business, large or small. A strategy will help you to see what you need to do and why you need to do it. Then, each action that you take will be more purposeful and effective.

For example, a strategy can help you to decide if you should open a retail store or an online store. The strategy will help you to develop your product lines and pricing strategies. It will also enable you to determine how many products you need to carry in inventory and when to buy more.

A good strategy will help you to determine whether or not you should buy additional equipment such as manufacturing equipment or whether to pay employees extra for overtime work instead of purchasing additional equipment. The strategy will also help you decide which employees are the most productive and what rewards are appropriate for them.

A good business strategy[79] will give your company direction, focus, and momentum toward the achievement of its objectives. When everyone in the company is always working from the same plan, each person becomes more effective than if he were working alone, and a good business strategy provides direction for your customers as well!

What are the factors that affect strategy?

---

[79] Business strategy, https://businessjargons.com/business-strategy.html

The success of any business strategy depends on the understanding of the factors that affect the strategy. There are six major factors:

Technological changes

The advent of the Internet is a good example. The Internet has changed how people communicate, find information, and how we do business.

For example, if you are a retail business, your customers will find you through the Internet. If you are a service provider, you will receive new customers through the Internet. If you want to compete in the future, paying attention to how technology affects your business is critical.

Social changes

The social climate has an impact on our daily lives, and often, it also affects the way we do business. For example, a negative political climate can affect consumer confidence, and they will be more careful with their money or may even refrain from spending it altogether. If you are a retailer, you have to be aware of these trends in order to survive in this changing environment.

For example, if the economy is bad, customers will be more price sensitive. If you want to stay in business, you have to adjust your strategy to the changing needs and demands of your customers.

Economic changes

In the same way that social changes can affect your business, economic changes can, too, such as interest rates and inflation rates, exchange rate fluctuations and other important criteria. If you own an import-export company, for example, you will have to adjust your prices accordingly when there are exchange rate fluctuations[80] between your country's currency and your export destination's currency. If you don't adjust your prices with these fluctuations, you will lose money by paying more for imported goods than what you charge for them when selling them locally or in another country.

For example, if you are importing goods from China to the US, any increase in the exchange rate between the U.S. dollar and the Chinese Yuan will cause you to pay more for a given amount of Chinese goods. In this case, you should increase your prices to compensate for any exchange rate changes.

Economic changes affect not only import/export businesses on a macro level, but it also affects small businesses in other ways such as increasing paper costs when there is an increase in oil prices or other raw material costs. Any of these changes may affect your business and its strategy.

Changes in consumer behavior

---

[80] Selwyn M.Gishen (updated January 7th 2021)
https://www.investopedia.com/ask/answers/08/how-often-to-exchange-rates-fluctuate.asp

Due to the increased number of products and services available on the marketplace, consumers are becoming more educated about their purchasing decisions. They are more demanding and rely less on traditional advertising methods to influence their buying decisions. Your product or service must stand out from that of all other competitors if you want to survive in this competitive environment. This is where a good strategy becomes vital for your success. The strategy should be able to differentiate your business from your competitors' by providing added value or by offering products/services that nobody else offers at present or in the near future. You have to be able to offer something special that will make people come back to you over and over again instead of going elsewhere when they need what you have to offer.

For example, say you own a retail business. You can offer free delivery of products to your customers. While other retailers might charge for this service, you offer it free of charge as a special bonus for buying your products. This will make your customers more loyal and will give them an additional reason to buy from you rather than from the other retailers in the marketplace.

Changes in the environment

Changes in environmental factors such as population growth, climate change, technological advances and other vital factors can affect your business. If you are selling food products and the weather changes and causes a shortage of certain types of food products in your area, you will have to make adjustments to your business strategy to accommodate the new situation. For example, you can change your product mix by adding new products that are more readily available or by reducing the number of products that are not available at present.

Another example is an increase in population growth. If you are a retail business, you will need to open new store locations to accommodate the growing population. Or if you are a service provider, you may need to hire more people or purchase additional equipment so that you can serve the growing population better.

Changes in laws and regulations

Laws and regulations can affect how your business operates. For example, if you are a retailer, you may need to change your business strategy if the state legislature passes a law requiring that all retailers charge the same price for goods sold.

The ability to identify what factors affect your business strategy will enable you to devise a plan that will lead your company to success.

How should a business select a strategy?

The strategy should be based on the company's mission statement and its goals. The business owner should decide what his or her goals are and then develop a strategy that will help him or her achieve those goals.

For example, if you want to make more money, you have to develop a strategy that will help you achieve that goal. You may need to change your marketing approach, advertise in different places, restructure your business model or change the products that you offer.

If your goal is to decrease expenses, you may need to downsize your staff, outsource some of your work or use a cheaper supplier. If your goal is to improve customer service, you may need to hire additional customer service representatives and train them on the phone skills needed for providing excellent customer service.

At times, business owners develop strategies without defining their ultimate goals. When this happens, the strategies are not effective because they do not lead toward a definite objective. There is no way to know if the overall plan is working because there is no specific goal against which they can be measured.

Take for example the owner of a restaurant who wants to increase sales. He decides to add a new menu item: beef bourguignon. The new menu item is a great idea for the restaurant, but will it necessarily lead to increased sales?

Without knowing the goal, you can't really know whether your strategy is working or not. A good strategy should be able to achieve the business owner's goals.

What is a good strategy?

A good strategy is a strategic plan that is both achievable and in alignment with the business and its values. It should also be realistic given the company's resources and capabilities and able to be implemented by the team.

What is the difference between a strategy, a plan, and an implementation plan?

A strategy describes the business's overarching goals. A plan describes how to achieve these goals, and an implementation plan is the "how" part of the plan.

Strategy should not be conflated with implementation; plans should not be used to describe strategy. Plans are for how to execute the strategy, while strategies are a statement of what should be achieved. In other words, strategies are about where to go, and plans are about how to get there.

For example, you could write a plan of how to go to the capital of Brazil. You could include information such as which roads to take, how much fuel to buy, and the best route from your current location.

However, this plan does not tell you where you are going—which is wrong, since you are trying to get to the Brazilian capital. To fix this problem, you would need a strategy that describes who/what is your target market (Brazilians), and why they should buy from you (because your product is amazing). The strategy will probably also describe how you will achieve your goal (sell on Amazon[81]).

---

[81] Amazon, https://www.amazon.in/

To execute the strategy, you need an implementation plan. This will be about how many products you want to sell each month, what price each should be sold at, and so on. When all this is done correctly, it should lead to achieving the goal stated in the strategy—which would be getting sales on Amazon.

Another example: If a person wants to lose weight in three months by eating less and exercising more, then she has given herself a goal and strategy for losing weight in three months by eating less sugar and exercising more. The person may have an implementation plan such as to eat less chocolate or walk an extra ten minutes every day. The person may also have a plan for how to get where she wants to be; for example, she may have a plan for what to eat if she goes out to eat with friends. The latter would not be a part of the strategy because it is not about what the person wants to achieve, but rather about how to get there.

In order for a strategy and implementation plan to work, they need to be realistic and achievable. This can be done by analyzing the strengths of the company, current resources and capabilities and potential threats and opportunities.

It can then be determined if the strategy and plans fit with the company's values and goals or capabilities. If all this has been considered, then the strategy should hopefully lead the company toward success in achieving its goals.

What are the elements of a good strategy?

A good strategy should have the following elements:

An overall objective

What should the business achieve in the long term (e.g., to be a leader in its category, to be profitable, to be the most loved chocolate brand)? This is sometimes called a vision or mission statement. For example, "We want to be the world's best chocolate brand."

A list of objectives

What specific things should the business do to achieve the overall objective (e.g., to be a leader in its category, to create great products and services, to increase sales by ten percent)? This is sometimes called a strategic plan or action plan. For example, to achieve our goal of being a leader in our category, we will increase sales by ten percent by launching new products, increasing price by five percent, improving quality and customer service).

The key success factors

What must the business do well in order for it to succeed (e.g., we need to deliver quality products at an affordable price; we must maintain high levels of quality; if we fail on any one of these, then we will not be successful)? Key success factors are often linked directly with strategies and objectives together, as this makes it easier for people within the organization to understand how they contribute toward achieving the company's goals. For example, our key success factors could be to develop and launch new products, increase sales by ten percent, maintain high levels of quality and improve customer service.

A list of tactical actions

How does a company achieve its goals? This is often called an action plan or implementation plan. For example, "We will develop new products over the next five years." This is usually divided into short-term actions (such as, "we will prepare a marketing plan within three months") and long-term actions. For example, "We will launch eight new products over the next five years."

Evaluation mechanisms

How does the organization know if it is achieving its objectives? For example, "We will evaluate our new products by measuring customer satisfaction." Evaluation mechanisms often form part of the action plans and are therefore closely linked to both the strategy and the objectives.

Cash flow

How much cash will be needed, from where and when? This can be referred to as a budget or financial plan[82].

---

[82] Julia Kagan (updated November 26th 2020)
https://www.investopedia.com/terms/f/financial_plan.asp

For example, "We will need $2 million from investors in order to launch our new products."

Threats

What could go wrong? For example, "What if we run out of cash?"

Opportunities

What opportunities does the business have if it does well in achieving its objectives and strategies? For example, "If we succeed in launching eight new products over the next five years, then we will be able to increase our market share significantly."

A list of assumptions

What must we believe is true if we are going to achieve our objectives? For example, "We must have excellent quality products." This can sometimes be difficult, as it is often hard to know if an assumption is true or false before trying something out. In reality, it is impossible not to have any assumptions, as you cannot prove them wrong until you see how things turn out. As such, assumptions should always be stated in terms of "we believe" or "we think" rather than in terms of fact. For example, "We believe/think that customers will like our new products once they try them."

Chapter 7: Entrepreneur Lifestyle

The lifestyle of an entrepreneur is a difficult one to describe. It can be exciting, rewarding and very challenging all at the same time. There is no typical day in the life of an entrepreneur.

A typical work week includes long hours and travel, but there are also moments of great satisfaction, joy and even excitement. The entrepreneur's lifestyle takes him or her to places not otherwise seen. It brings new knowledge and insight into people's lives and brings up problems that need solutions. This lifestyle provides unique opportunities for solving problems in many different ways—ways that might not be possible for someone who works within the framework of a large company's bureaucracy.

Entrepreneurship is a way of life defined by extraordinary accomplishments. It is marked by creativity, tenacity, hard work and risk-taking—just to name a few character traits that are required to make it successful. And all these factors bring rewards beyond imagination as well as some risks which most people will never experience firsthand.

In this chapter, we will discuss some of the basic lifestyle issues that are especially relevant to business owners from both a personal and financial viewpoint.

Dream Big and Start Small

The first thing you need to do is develop a vision of what your business will be like in the future. What does it look like? How big will it be? What kind of market share will you have? What kind of profits will you make?

It is important to visualize how things will look down the road so that you can be motivated and enthusiastic toward reaching those goals. It also helps to keep you on track and focused on what needs to be done today to reach them in the future. Otherwise, the day-to-day operations of a small business may seem too mundane to get excited about, and you may lose focus and motivation.

You need to see where you are headed and why. To do this, first envision yourself as a successful entrepreneur, with all the trappings that go along with it—lots of money in your pocket, freedom from rigid schedules, flexibility in how you do things, and other perks of the job. This vision is vital because it creates an image that can help motivate you when times get tough. If we didn't have dreams for our lives—if we were satisfied being mediocre—then most people would never push themselves beyond their comfort zone toward achieving their dreams. So, start by dreaming big!

For example, let's say you want to start your own business, and you're not quite sure how to do it. You've tried a few things on your own, but nothing has worked out yet. The main reason may be that you don't have a clear vision of what the business will look like or how it will operate. You may picture yourself as an entrepreneur who runs a successful business—but you don't know what that means. So how do you get there?

Start by thinking about a few key elements that all successful businesses share:

1. A product or service that people want or need. This is the core of every business and is what differentiates it from every other company in its industry.
2. A plan for getting the word out about your product/service so that people know about it. In other words, you need to develop an effective marketing strategy. This is very important because if no one knows about your product or service, then no one can buy it.
3. A good idea of where to find customers for your product or service—i.e., who buys the product/service? Who is your target market? These are known as "target market characteristics."
4. A way of producing and distributing your product or service. How will you deliver it to your customers? Who will manufacture it? Where will you produce it? These are known as "operational factors."

These four elements are the critical components of any successful business. If you can figure out how to incorporate them into the business model, then you have a very good chance of success.

Be the Boss of Yourself

One of the most important things for an entrepreneur to understand is that he or she is the boss of himself or herself. There are no employers to check up on you. There are no managers to assign work to you or tell you what to do. You are your boss—and you alone are responsible for your success or failure.

Being the boss of yourself means that you have complete control over how much you do and how hard you will work, what hours you keep and how much time off you take. You can choose what projects to work on and which ones not to work on. You can choose which customers will get your attention and which ones will not be a priority for you at this time. You can decide whether or not a particular project is worth pursuing, based on your interest level in it, as well as your assessment of its potential reward vs. risk ratio— regardless of what other people may think about it.

Your business will be successful if it makes money because of your efforts alone and not because of any decisions made by others who report to someone else who reports up the chain of command until they reach someone who has authority over them. If your business relies too much on others for it to make money, it is not a good business. It is essential for you to be an entrepreneur, not an employee working for someone who is the boss of you.

If you are like most entrepreneurs, your business will make you money because of the decisions that you make. It will be a reflection of your creativity, skills, talents and efforts. No one else can take credit for any success or failure of your business but yourself. Even if others are helping in some way, they are only giving their time and efforts to help make your business more successful because it benefits them in some way—whether they work for you or not.

Therefore, the lifestyle of an entrepreneur must include accepting full responsibility for his or her success and facing the consequences of his or her actions directly without blaming others for problems that arise from these actions. This includes all aspects of daily living—not just business activities but how much work one does each day versus how much time off one takes, how healthy versus unhealthy one is, what food one eats, how much money versus debt one accumulates and other personal factors. In other words, whatever happens to you is a reflection of yourself alone—on all levels personal and professional. This seems very basic, but many entrepreneurs fail to grasp this concept and thus fail to accept responsibility for the consequences of their actions.

If you do not want to accept full responsibility for your life, then you are not ready to be an entrepreneur, and you should consider working for someone else. This will be a difficult thing for many people to accept, but it is a necessary thing if one wants to succeed as an entrepreneur.

Entrepreneurship is Investing in Yourself First

To succeed, an entrepreneur must be willing to invest in him-or-herself. This does not mean spending a lot of money on yourself. The opposite is true. Being an entrepreneur means long-term spending money on your business before you see any income. It means taking the long-term view so that you can reap the benefits of your efforts in the future. It means continually learning new skills so that you can do a better job and earn more money, and it means investing in your employees by providing them with opportunities for learning and growth as well as good pay and benefits.

One of the biggest challenges facing entrepreneurs is that they often don't have enough money to invest in their businesses or themselves—at least in the beginning. They are usually bootstrapping—trying to build up their businesses with limited resources and without outside help. This is another reason why it is important to be sure that you have a solid business plan before you start on your entrepreneurial journey!

To become successful as an entrepreneur, then you need to be able to overcome your fear of spending money before seeing returns on it—even if this means living on a shoestring budget for a while. You need to take risks and invest in your ideas and yourself without knowing whether they will provide a return. You will not be able to do this unless you are positive that the money you invest is well spent—and that it is money that you don't need to have in the short term.

You also need to develop a long-term view of your business. You must plot out what needs to be done and how it can be done so that you can focus on the future instead of obsessing about the present. If you can do this, you can overcome your fears of risk-taking and failure which will allow you to take advantage of opportunities as they arise.

There are many ways to overcome your fears of risk-taking and failure. One is by developing good business skills and getting good advice from people who know what they're doing. Another is by learning how to handle problems or failures that arise so they don't stop your progress or send you back a few steps.

Another way of overcoming these fears is by having a very strong belief in yourself and what you are doing—even if others have doubts about it! Having confidence in yourself will help you realize that when things go wrong, it's not the end of the world. it will also help you realize that risk-taking is not about taking risks just for the sake of taking risks, but about doing what needs to be done to make your business a success.

Being an entrepreneur also means being willing to invest in the lives of others. It means being willing to devote time and money to training and mentoring your employees so that they can become successful in their own right. It also means being able to reach out to other people who are willing to help you succeed, whether it's through lending a helping hand or by providing financial assistance.

It means being able to commit yourself wholeheartedly to yourself and your company instead of spreading yourself thin by trying to do too many things at once. It means being able to say no when you need extra time for work or family— and then not feeling bad about it later because you've let someone else down or let go of an opportunity that turned out not so great anyway!

Finally, entrepreneurship is about investing in new ideas and new ways of thinking whenever they come along. You need the vision and belief in yourself and your company that will allow you to recognize opportunities that others might miss or overlook—especially if those opportunities involve changing existing ways of doing things.

With this in mind, let's turn to some specific lifestyle issues that you will face as an entrepreneur.

The Emotion of Entrepreneurship

Every entrepreneur is different. Some are outgoing and talkative; others are quiet and reflective. But all share a common trait—their enthusiasm for their business ideas.

The challenge of entrepreneurship is like a drug; it can be addictive. All entrepreneurs feel the same sense of excitement about their business ideas as they grow beyond the initial stage. This is especially true when the business begins to achieve some success, which means that it will keep growing and expanding, creating new growth opportunities.

Do many entrepreneurs have difficulty defining exactly what drives them to do what they do—the challenge of creating something out of nothing, with little or no help from anyone else? Is it money? Or is it the ability to see something that no one else can see? Perhaps it's just a combination of all these factors plus many more that make up the love of entrepreneurship itself.

Entrepreneurs also tend to be risk-takers in everything they do—even in their personal lives. Their conversations often include stories about how they overcame obstacles and took risks that most people would consider foolish or reckless.

But for an entrepreneur, taking risks is part of everyday life; risk-taking becomes a part of your attitude toward life itself.

Despite their single-minded focus on their business ventures, entrepreneurs also have a strong desire to be independent and self-reliant. This is especially true of the entrepreneur who works alone. But even for the entrepreneur who has a business partner, there is still an intense need to be self-reliant.

Another common trait of entrepreneurs is that they are usually very individualistic. They believe that they can make it on their own—and they usually do! This independence and sense of self-sufficiency become part of the entrepreneur's identity. It becomes a central part of the person's ego or sense of self.

Of course, it's one thing to know about these common traits and another thing entirely to experience them yourself. The only way you can learn about what it means to be an entrepreneur is by doing it yourself—by taking the challenges, risks, and rewards that come with running your own business.

The Law of Attraction

The Law of Attraction[83] states that energy flows where attention goes. If you want to be rich, then your thoughts and focus must be on how to become rich. If you want to be healthy, then your thoughts and focus must be on how to keep yourself healthy. If you want to experience love in your life,

---

[83] **Elizabeth Scott**, https://www.verywellmind.com/understanding-and-using-the-law-of-attraction-3144808

then your thoughts and focus must be on how to attract the love that you desire.

If you think about being poor or destitute, that is what will happen. You will attract poverty into your life. On the other hand, if you think about being prosperous and successful in life, then those things will come into your life as well. Think about what you would like to attract into your life, and you will find that it will come.

If you are unemployed and have been out of work for a while, then focus on how to find a job. If you are already employed but want to find a better job with more pay, then focus on finding such a job. If you want to start your own business, then focus on that goal as well.

There is no doubt that the individual who focuses on the goal he or she desires will achieve it sooner than those who don't focus on it. And that extra drive and determination will help ensure that it happens even sooner than if they did not have those qualities.

For business owners, the Law of Attraction is especially important. If you are not focused on your business and how to make it more successful, then it is likely that your business will suffer. Think about ways to improve your business, and focus on those improvements. Think about how to increase sales, profits, and the value of your business—then focus on achieving those goals. If you don't focus on the success of your business, you may find yourself in financial trouble. If that happens, then you might have to close down shop or sell out.

The Sacrifices

Owning your own business is rewarding, but it also has inherent risks and sacrifices. One of the biggest sacrifices is time. No matter what business you are in, you will need to spend a significant amount of time running the business and not as much time doing the other things in life that you enjoy doing. Being an entrepreneur is like juggling many balls at once.

You need to keep your attention focused on all different aspects of your business. For example, you need to keep your eyes on both the short-term and long-term goals simultaneously. You need to balance cash flow with growth goals while deciding how much money to pay yourself each month versus how much money should go back into the business for growth or new projects. These are just a few examples of what you must deal with on any given day (or week). Do not expect this lifestyle to be easy, as it is very demanding and requires a lot of hard work.

The Unexpected

Another sacrifice that most entrepreneurs make is that they have less "down time" than people who work for others do. Because of this, they rarely have set schedules and may have little control over their daily routines. This can be partly attributed to the uncertainty of most businesses.

Entrepreneurs have to work around the unexpected and often spend more time on "unplanned" projects than they would like. They may work long hours to get their jobs done on time. Also, as a business owner, you have to deal with many more things at once than you did as an employee. You must be able to handle multiple tasks at the same time.

Being a business owner also involves longer work hours and more stress than the average job does. The uncertainty of running your own business can cause anxiety, which can take a toll on both your physical health and mental well-being. At times you may feel overwhelmed by all that goes into running your own company; especially in the early years when you are still learning how to grow the business and make it successful. This is not for everyone! But if you are an entrepreneur at heart, then this will be rewarding for you over time as your business becomes bigger and you manage it better.

Financial Sacrifices

Money is another sacrifice[84] that entrepreneurs make more often than employees do. Since most businesses are funded by personal cash flows or bank loans, there is very little room for error if things don't go according to plan or if your business is not as profitable as you had originally hoped.

One thing that will help reduce your financial risks is to have a sound business plan in place before you start your company. A business plan will help you keep track of the finances of the company regularly and also give you a clear picture of what has worked and what hasn't worked for your

---

[84] **Ben Kingsley,** https://empowerwealth.com.au/blog/financial-sacrifices-and-choices/

business in the past. You can always make changes to your original plan, but at least having one will get you organized and thinking about how to make each aspect more successful than it was in the past.

Financial sacrifices are another part of being an entrepreneur that shouldn't be overlooked, since most people don't think about them until they are faced with them. If you aren't prepared for this before starting your business, then this may be very difficult for you when it comes time to make some hard choices about things like "Do I pay my mortgage or do I pay my employees?" or, "Do I buy a new car or hire some new sales staff?" These types of decisions are part of life as an entrepreneur. Money isn't infinite, so you will need to make decisions which inevitably means that sometimes things won't go exactly according to how you would have liked them to.

Now that we have gone through the lifestyle of the entrepreneur, we will talk about some basic business fundamentals that business owners need to understand to start and operate a successful business.

Chapter 8: 26 Best Practices & Tips

As a business owner, you are faced with many challenges and can get overwhelmed. You may have the best product or service in the world, but if you do not run your business right, you will not be successful. This chapter has many tips and tricks that you can apply to your business. These are proven tips that have been used by other successful business owners.

When you are new to the world of business, you can get caught up in the fast-paced lifestyle and lose focus. You may want to try every new marketing strategy or product, but you need to have a solid foundation. The best way to do this is to learn from the past and the experience and outcome of other business ventures. Look at what has worked for other companies that are similar to yours, and adapt it for your needs.

Here are some of the best practices and tips collated and summarized from the experience and advice taken from the best entrepreneurs for new business owners.

Focus on One Thing

One of the things that can kill a business is getting too many things going at once. It can be difficult to focus on one product or service when you have so many ideas. You may want to try them all out, but this can take your eye off the ball.

It is better to focus on one or two and use them to drive your business growth.

As a business owner, you should focus on what you are good at and improve it. If you are not good at marketing, then hire someone who is an expert in the field. It is better to have one or two things that are well done than a great number of things done poorly.

For example, if you are starting a software company, focus on one piece of software that you can market to everyone. If you have multiple pieces of software that do the same thing, you will not know which one to push the hardest. You will get lost in your own product line and may even lose a customer once they see the same product in another niche.

Learn from the Past

It is important to learn from mistakes that others have made. If you are a new business owner, it is critical that you learn from other successful business owners. There may be some ideas that have worked for years but are now obsolete. As the world changes and technology advances, your business has to evolve and change as well. Look at previous ideas and adapt them for today's world if they still work.

You can learn from other successful businesses in many ways. You can read about them on the Internet or speak with someone who works there. You should also look at how they market their products and what types of services they offer customers. This will give you an idea of what works best in your industry and help you decide where you should focus your marketing efforts.

For example, if a company has been around for 50 years and is still doing well, then there must be something working right for them. This could be the type of product they offer or how they advertise it to customers. You could look at their marketing techniques to see what works best for your business or even copy them directly if you think it will benefit your company as well.

Understand Your Market

Before you start your business, you need to know your market. This means that you have to understand the demographics of your customers and the people that are most likely to buy your product or service. If you do not know who your customers are, then it will be difficult for you to market to them. This is why many companies hire marketing agencies or consultants in order to help them determine their target market.

For example, if you are selling children's clothes online, it is important that you focus on parents with small kids or babies. If they do not have children, then they will not be a potential customer. You may want to expand your target market later on down the road, but it is important that you start off with a clear understanding of who you are offering products and services to.

Start Small

When you start a new business, it can be tempting to grow quickly and take over the world. You may want to open a new store every week or add more products as soon as possible. It can be difficult for business owners who want everything right now to think about tomorrow when there is so much success available today. However, the best way to ensure long-term success is by starting small and building up your business.

Growing too quickly can lead to lots of problems in your company. For example, if you have a large number of employees but not enough products to sell, you will lose money. If you do not have enough money coming in, you will not be able to pay your employees, and they will leave. This is why it is important to start off with a small business plan and stick with it until it starts to work for you.

For example, if you are starting a clothing store, open with two or three employees and a small shop. If you have an excellent product that people want, it will start to sell itself as word-of-mouth spreads quickly. As the store starts making money, grow your staff and expand the store by adding more space or another location. This is how most successful businesses grow, and there are many examples of companies who started this way and are still in business today.

Stay Organized

As the owner of a business, there are many tasks that need to be completed each day including bookkeeping, inventory control, employee management and so many other important tasks. Managing all of these tasks can be difficult for even the most organized person. However, if you are not organized, your business will suffer.

You should spend a few hours each week organizing and planning ahead. This way you can save time by not having to make decisions all of the time and you will also be able to keep track of what is happening in the company. When employees are working on certain tasks, they should also follow a schedule that is organized. This way everyone knows what they need to do and when they need to do it by.

If you are disorganized, you will not be able to run your business properly and it will affect your bottom line profits. Your customers may get upset if they have to wait too long for service or help from employees because there is no set schedule for them. You may even lose employees if they cannot handle the organization of your team. As a result, it is crucial for business owners to stay organized and have a plan if they want their businesses to grow.

Learn from Your Mistakes

It is natural for errors and mistakes to occur within every business at some point in time. When these mistakes happen, do not dwell on them or become frustrated with yourself because this can harm your business in the long run.

Instead, try to learn from these mistakes and prevent them from happening again.

For example, if you make a mistake that costs your business a lot of money, think about how you can prevent it from happening again. You may have to change certain policies or the way that you run your company. Maybe you need to hire more employees, so that everyone follows the same rules and regulations. Whatever the error is, try to find a solution that will help fix it and keep it from reoccurring in the future.

During your first few years of business, you will make mistakes, and it is okay. Just make sure to learn from them, and do not repeat them again in the future. If you are able to do this, then your business will grow stronger than ever before!

Know Your Customers

When you own a business, it is important to know your customers. You should know what they want and need and the best way to reach them. If you do not know your customers, then you will have a difficult time marketing your products or services.

For example, if you are selling clothing in a mall, you should know the types of people that shop there. This way you can target certain demographics with your marketing campaigns and products. For example, if most of your customers are teenagers and young adults, then your ads should reflect this such as using people who are young in the advertisements or having funny slogans on the clothing that appeal to younger demographics. If most of your customers are older adults who have kids, then you can add family friendly slogans on the clothing that use words like "we" instead of "I'm" or "our" instead of "my." Using these simple changes can really help increase sales among certain demographics!

If you do not know who your customers are, it will be hard to market to them effectively. You will not be able to tell which demographic is buying most of your products or why they are not purchasing certain things. As a result, you will not be able to create effective marketing campaigns and your sales will suffer. So, make sure to know your customers and what they need so that you can sell more products!

Focus on Success

As a business owner, it is important to focus on success more than anything else. If you can focus on your goals in life and the direction that you want to go in, then it will be easier for you to achieve them. Your vision of success should always be in front of you so that you can see what is coming next.

However, keep in mind that each day will have its own challenges and obstacles that are trying to pull you off course. When this happens, do not give up, but instead work harder until they are overcome. If something bad happens at work or with your business, do not let it get the best of you, but instead think about how you can overcome it and move forward. The key is always trying harder than before and refusing to give up when times get tough!

For example, one day while running a successful business may mean working two extra hours after normal business hours or staying an hour late every day until the job is done. If you are the type of person that gives up when the going gets tough, then you will not be able to achieve your goals.

Do Not Give Up

Doing something new for the first time can be scary and intimidating. For example, if you are a business owner and have never done any marketing, it can be very challenging to try it for the first time. You may be afraid of failure or that you will spend a lot of money with no results. However, if you give up before trying, then it will never happen!

Instead, take small steps to overcome these fears and get started. For example, do some research on how to market your product or service online or even just how to set up an email account. Once you have mastered this small task, it will become easier for you to move on to bigger things. In fact, once you see one small step being completed successfully, it is easier for you to take action on other tasks in your business. This is because it builds your confidence in your abilities as a business owner and shows that what may seem tough at first is actually fairly easy with a little effort!

Keep Your Eye on the Prize

As a business owner, nothing else matters except your goals and that you are working toward them. Your family, friends, and social life will take a back seat for now because you need to focus on your goals. This may seem like a very bad thing, but it is actually healthy to not be distracted by other things in your life and just stay focused on the task at hand.

For example, as a business owner you have to put in long hours sometimes if you want to make it big. This might mean that you have to miss family events or go out with friends less often than normal. However, do not feel guilty or worry about this because these sacrifices are necessary if you want to achieve the ultimate goal of success. Remember that your business will always be there and so will your family and friends!

Get New Ideas

When running a successful business, it is important to always be looking for new ideas that can help improve your business. You should never stop looking for new ways to improve your products, services, or even how you run things in the office! This is because even though one idea may work well today, there are many changes happening around us all the time, and it may not work tomorrow.

For example, if you have a successful marketing plan today, this does not mean that it will always work for you. This is because the Internet is always changing, and new trends or technology are always popping up. Therefore, this means that your marketing plan will also need to change along with it.

Delegate Work to Get More Done

Many business owners love to do everything themselves. They like to be in control and make all the decisions. While there is nothing wrong with this, it will slow you down. You can get more done when you delegate work to your employees and let them take the reins. They are motivated to do a good job for you, and they will look for ways to improve your business.

This does not mean you should sit back and relax while they work, though. You need to know how things are going in your company so that you can coach them on their tasks. You should meet with them regularly so they can update you on what is going on in the company and ask questions about how they can improve their performance. This is a great way to motivate your employees as well as keep tabs on the business's productivity.

For example, you could create a scorecard that they fill out with all the tasks they completed each day. At the end of each week, you can review their work and give them some suggestions for improvement. This helps them get better at what they are doing and motivates them to do a better job. In most cases, this will help them become more productive and reach their goals quicker.

Incentives for Employees

It is important to motivate your employees, especially if you are trying to get them to do something they have not done before. If you want your employees to learn a new marketing strategy, you can create a contest where the winner gets a cash bonus or other prize. This will make them more excited about learning how to do it and it will motivate your employees as well. You should also reward employees when they complete certain tasks by giving them raises or giving them time off from work. You never know how these bonuses or incentives will affect your business if you never try it out!

Effective Time Management

When managing your business, it is important to be organized so that you can manage your time efficiently. As an entrepreneur[85], you have many responsibilities within the company that need to be taken care of on a daily basis. You should create a schedule and stick to it. You will be able to do this by creating a daily schedule of the most important tasks that need to be completed. This will allow you to check off each task as it is completed to keep track of what needs to be done each day.

You should also spend time each day planning for the upcoming days and week. This way, you can keep track of what needs to get done and prioritize your activities. If you do not

---

[85] Adam Hayes (updated February 26th 2021)
https://www.investopedia.com/terms/e/entrepreneur.asp

plan ahead, you could get caught in a hectic pace where things fall through the cracks.

For example, you could create a list of what needs to get done each day and week. This is a great way to manage your time and keep track of everything that needs to be completed. You should also spend time planning for the upcoming days and week. Make sure you have scheduled breaks in between your daily tasks so that you can get some rest. As the business owner, you need to be able to think clearly in order to make good decisions. You can't do this if you are tired and stressed out all the time!

Remain Professional

It is important for you as the owner of your business to remain professional at all times. This will help you gain respect from your employees as well as other business owners around town. If you act like a loose cannon, it will hurt your reputation and decrease productivity in your company. People like doing business with those who they feel they can trust and rely on for help when needed. By keeping a professional attitude, it will show that there is no need for them to be worried about asking for help or assistance from you or your employees when needed.

You should also make sure that everyone working in your company dresses professionally as well. It is important that people respect how the staff of your company presents themselves. This will show that you take pride in your work and it will help everyone get along better with each other.

When in Doubt, Ask for Help

When starting your business, you may have many questions and feel alone. It is important to get assistance from people who have been in your shoes before. There are many entrepreneurs that can help you throughout the process, especially with the legal aspects of starting a business.

The first time I started a business, I didn't know any lawyers[86]. As I was getting ready to open the doors to my new business, I felt like I was going to be in over my head. Luckily for me, there was someone who helped me with all of my legal issues and got everything together for me. He also gave me some great tips on how to run a successful business.

If you are lucky enough to have someone like this in your life, take advantage of it! If not, consider hiring someone that specializes in helping small businesses get off the ground. You don't want to miss out on using all of the tools available to you because you don't know what they are or how they work!

Learn How to Hire Great Employees

Having great employees is key when it comes to running a successful business. The right employees can make even the worst product look amazing with their stellar customer service.

---

[86] **Joseph Haddad,** https://www.jjh-law.com/what-does-a-business-lawyer-do/

When hiring employees, there are two traits you need to look for in a person: 1) they have a good attitude, and 2) they love your product or service. If you have someone who does not like your business, they will not be happy, and it will reflect in their work.

The most important skill you need to look for when hiring an employee is communication skills. If an employee cannot communicate with your customers, they will not be happy and neither will your customers! Make sure all of your employees know how to speak and write clearly so that you can convey the message that you want to send out.

There is no one-size-fits-all formula for hiring great employees, but there are some great resources available on the Internet that can help you find the right people for the job! One site I use, found at www.indeed.com, allows me to search by keyword or location for people who have specific skills I need! This way I can cut down on my time searching for the right candidate and save time recruiting new employees.

Consistency is Key

Once you have made a decision, stick to it. This is something that happens much more frequently in a small business. You are better able to see how a decision is affecting the business. When you have a team of employees, it can be harder to see how the decision you made is affecting them. You may not even realize they are unhappy with what you have done until it is too late.

Consistency can also impact your customers. They come to expect certain things from your business, and when you change it up, they will feel like something is wrong. They do not know what was changed or why, but they are upset about it anyway. Consistency builds trust and a relationship in your business over time.

For example, if you have an online store and you run your business well, you will see a regular stream of customers. These customers will expect certain things from your business. They may expect to get a response to their email within 24 hours, or they may see the products that they want in your store every time they visit. If you don't respond to their emails right away or update your site every other week, they will not be happy with your business anymore.

If you make a decision that impacts one of these expectations, keep it consistent. Consistency gains trust over time and builds a relationship between your customers and your business. This is something that you want to work hard on maintaining.

Be a Leader and Not a Micromanager

A lot of smaller businesses are run by the one and only owner. This can be good because you have complete control, but it can also be bad because you have to do everything yourself.

One of the biggest things that a small business needs is a leader. The person who is leading the company should be up-front with everyone, telling them what is expected of them.

The leader should also be able to delegate tasks to others. If you cannot trust your employees to do their job right, they will not work as hard as they could, and your business will suffer. A good leader will know when employees are doing well and reward them accordingly.

The leader should also be able to hold their employees accountable for their work. If an employee is not doing their job or is slacking off, the leader needs to step in and make sure that they do what needs to be done or fire them if necessary. You may think that it's better to give employees second chances, but you will just end up hurting your business in the long run if you allow employees to slack off without consequence. It comes down to trust, and if you don't trust your employee enough to do their job, then they need a new job! It is better to have one or two employees who work hard and are productive than a whole team of slackers.

The leader should also be able to spot new opportunities and know when to make changes. If there is something that is not working in your business, the leader needs to step in and fix it. A leader will be able to make your business more successful more quickly than a micromanager could ever do!

Know Your Numbers

The best way to keep an eye on your business is through tracking your numbers. There are many different ways you can do this, and it is a good idea to keep a budget spreadsheet[87]. You should have a plan in place for both your short term and long-term goals[88]. This way, if you are not meeting your goals, you can figure out why and make adjustments as needed. If you do not know your numbers, then you will not be able to make the proper adjustments when needed.

The most common number that is tracked is the money coming in and going out of your company. You should keep a close eye on your income, expenses and profits. You should also keep track of things like employee turnover. If you have high turnover, then you need to figure out why that is happening and make adjustments as needed. Keep track of how many hours each employee works each week.

Another thing you should keep track of is your inventory levels. This will help you avoid running out of products or having too much inventory. You will be able to see if there are certain products that need to be reordered more often or if there are certain products that no one seems to want on a regular basis. This will help you figure out what items need to stay on the shelves and which ones need to go.

---

[87] Budget spreadsheet,
https://corporatefinanceinstitute.com/resources/templates/excel-modeling/personal-budget-spreadsheet
[88] Long term goals,
https://careerwise.minnstate.edu/mymncareers/english-learner/long-term-goal.html

If you keep these numbers organized, it will be easier for you to see where your time needs to be spent on a daily basis. Your time is valuable, so it is important that it is spent wisely on tasks that can benefit your business the most. If you spend too much time trying to implement marketing strategies that do not work or trying new products, then your business will suffer because there are other areas in which you need to attend.

Build a Strong Team Around You

How can you be successful without a strong team? Whether it's your employees or your network of investors, you need people around you to help you. A good team will always support and help each other succeed. When you have a strong team around you, it will make running your business more comfortable, and you will not have to do it alone.

It would help if you built relationships with other business owners in your industry. They probably have dealt with very similar situations and can give you great advice. You can also learn from their mistakes so you can avoid them yourself. For example, there may be a new marketing strategy working for a few of your competitors that you want to try out. You will want to talk to them first because they may have tried a strategy that did not work well, or they discovered something about the product that you are not aware of.

You can also ask for help from your employees. You will want to ask them what their goals are and how you can help them achieve them. They may not have the same goals as you do, so make sure they know what it takes to get to the next level. It would help if you also asked your employees how they think you can improve your business and how they feel about your business's direction.

Another great way to build a team is to network with other businesses and organizations in your industry. Networking allows you to learn from other people's experiences, and you can even find new regular customers or investors. Most of the time, networking will lead to great opportunities that could not have been found in any other way.

Have a Strong Foundation

Every business, no matter how big or small, needs a solid foundation. This means building systems that you can follow each day to make your business successful. Even if the company is fool-proof, if you do not build strategies around it, someone else will take over and run it better than you ever could! It's better to create a fail-proof foundation so that your company will run smoothly with little effort on your part! That way, when you do leave, someone else can take over and continue running things as good as they were before! The best way to start building a foundation is with a business plan. This is an outline of your business strategy and will tell you how you want to run it. This is very important and helps keep you on track.

Build Trust

Trust is crucial when running a business because it is essential for long-term success. When you build trust with your customers, employees, and investors, you must be honest with them and be consistent in everything you do. Everyone on your team must be on the same page because this will enable them to work better together. This means that everyone must know what is expected of them when they work with someone else or perform their job duties at work.

A great way to build trust is to show people that your business's future is in their hands. By giving them a sense of ownership, you build trust because they know that you are just as invested in the industry as they are. This also shows them that you believe in them and will not blame them if something goes wrong. It is also a good idea to have your employees help with your social media accounts or help with the business's marketing strategies. This will give them a sense of ownership and make them feel like they are part of the team.

It would help if you always were consistent and honest when dealing with others outside of your business. Always deliver on time and what you promise to provide. It would help if you never lied about anything because it will eventually come out at some point and may even affect your business relationships negatively. It's also essential that you remain consistent with how you deal with customers, employees, investors, and suppliers. This can confuse them when they do not know how you will act in different situations or circumstances.

It would be best if you always made yourself available to your employees, family, and others you are in business with. When people have questions for you, they should be able to contact you whenever they need to. If they cannot reach you, they may feel as if their problems are unimportant. This will make them feel as if they are not part of the team and make them think that it is okay not to put in 100% effort when working on a project.

Also, there may be times when people need your help with something outside of work. If your employees trust you and know that you care about them as people, they will be more likely to help out in a time of need. You should always be there for others no matter what the situation is. Not only does this build trust, but it can also build loyalty from others around you.

Be Disciplined

Discipline is essential when you are running a business. Like any other job, you need to be on time every day and be prepared for your meetings and other important events. This means that you should know what tasks need to be completed by a specific time and when they must be completed. You should also always stay organized because this will help you run your business more efficiently. This is especially important because you will have fewer distractions when you are organized.

You should always set goals that are realistic and achievable for your business. Thus, it is good to break big tasks into smaller ones so it does not seem overwhelming anymore. If you do set goals that are too big, it may discourage your employees from working as hard as possible because they feel like their efforts are not making a difference in the company's overall success rate. If your employees do not feel like their hard work is making a difference, then they will probably leave the company or become less productive in their work duties.

You should develop solid habits for yourself so that every day is productive for your business. When creating patterns, make sure that they fit into your lifestyle instead of changing everything to do your business. For example, you may want to wake up an hour earlier and work on your business before you go to work. This is a great way to get a head start on your tasks every day, but it may not be realistic for everyone.

You should also make sure that you plan for your business's future so that you are always prepared for anything that happens. You should have a plan in place if one of your suppliers goes out of business or if one of your employees leaves the company. Having a backup plan will help you remain calm, relaxed, and collected when these situations occur. It would help if you also created a financial plan because it will help you make better decisions with money.

Follow the Golden Rule

The Golden Rule is one of the most basic rules in life, but it can help your business in many ways. Always treat others how you would like to be treated, and this will keep everyone happy with how things are run in your company or business. There are some basic examples of the Golden Rule. Treat everyone with respect, do not lie to anyone, give back to the community, treat your employees with respect and care about them as people and always do your best.

Always be honest with your employees and customers. If you make a mistake, do not try to cover it up or make excuses for it. Just admit that you made a mistake, and explain what happened so they are not in the dark about anything. This will also show your employees that you are human and make mistakes just like anyone else. Everyone makes mistakes sometimes, but how people deal with their mistakes says a lot about them. In business, everyone must trust one another because this will allow everyone to work more efficiently together.

Asking for help is one of the best ways to build trust and relationships with people around you. People are much more likely to help someone who asks for help instead of someone who does not ask for any assistance at all. You can do this by asking questions to learn more about what they do. For example, if you have a new employee in your company that works on marketing strategies, ask them what their favorite marketing strategy is or how they feel about the newest social media platform out there. By doing this, they know that you are interested in their opinion and that you are not just asking them for information for the sake of it.

Focus on the Customer

Customer service is something that sets your business apart from others. If you are not paying attention to customer service, people will not return to your store or buy your products. People will also tell their friends and family about how they were treated, which can negatively affect your business.

The best way to ensure good customer service is to make sure everyone on your team fully understands what the company goals are, and then make sure that they know what they have to do to achieve them. It would help if you always treated everyone fairly regardless of their position or rank within the company because this will help keep morale up, and it will show your customers that you care about them as people.

Every person matters at your company, so treat everyone equally and fairly when dealing with them. If someone has a problem, address it as soon as possible so they do not have any problems with the product or service that you provided. If someone complains about a product or service, take note of it and find out what went wrong so you can fix it before it happens again. The best way to fix a problem is to address it right away and make sure that it does not happen again.

Always make sure that you are providing your customers with quality products and services. If your products or services are not the best quality, people will not return to your business because they will be going to a competitor who offers better quality. It's also essential to provide excellent customer service to keep your customers coming back for more. If you can do this, you will have loyal customers that will tell their friends about your company.

When running a business, the most important thing is making sure that you are putting out high-quality products or services. You should never offer lower quality products or services than what is expected of you because it can hurt your business' reputation, and you could possibly even go out of business if people are not happy with the work they receive from you.

One way to ensure good customer service is to train everyone on how to treat customers. This means training them on how they should greet the customer, answer the phone, and what product or service they need when someone calls in for help. If everyone knows what needs to be done, it will make things easier for them and will increase the amount of satisfaction the customer has.

Another great way to ensure good customer service is to make sure that your employees understand their job duties. If they know what they are supposed to do, it will make things easier for them, and they will be able to do a better job of providing excellent customer service. It would help if you also had them go through training on how to treat customers to understand better what you expect from them. You should also make sure that you provide them with ongoing training to continue to learn new things.

If you provide excellent customer service, your customers will keep coming back and tell their friends how great your business is. If you provide poor customer service, your business reputation can go down the drain, and you may end up losing customers or going out of business altogether. Always focus on the quality of your products or services and the work you put out because this really matters in the long run.

Conclusion

We have come to the end of this book. We have discussed in depth the basics of business. Now it's your turn to start your own business and make it a success. I hope you learned a lot from the book and apply those learnings in your life to achieve success.

The most important thing about building a business is to have a clear plan of action. When you have a clear plan, it will be easier for you to define your goals and the steps you need to achieve them. It's important to remember that running a business isn't easy, but if you do it right, then it might be gratifying. If you want to succeed in your venture, you should write down a strategy to make the business profitable.

In this book, we have discussed some of the most important things you should keep in mind if you want your business to succeed. It's essential to know what your goals are and how you can achieve them. You should also know how much money you will need for your business to have a clear vision. Once you have these things in place, then it will be easier for you to get started.

The next step is up to you! Good luck!

www.ingramcontent.com/pod-product-compliance
Lightning Source LLC
Chambersburg PA
CBHW071233210326
41597CB00016B/2030